a taste of
sunshine
jenny bristow

BLACKSTAFF
PRESS

BELFAST

IN ASSOCIATION WITH UTV

contents

snacks and soups

fish

meat

desserts

conversion tables

volume

1 tsp	5ml
1 dsp	10ml
1 tbsp	15ml
55ml	2floz
75ml	3floz
125ml	4floz
150ml	$^1/4$pt
275ml	$^1/2$pt
425ml	$^3/4$pt
570ml	1pt
1 litre	$1^3/4$pt

oven temperatures

degrees centigrade	gas mark
140°	1
150°	2
170°	3
180°	4
190°	5
200°	6
220°	7
230°	8
240°	9

weights

grams	ounces
10g	$^1/2$oz
25g	1oz
40g	$1^1/2$oz
50g	2oz
60g	$2^1/2$oz
75g	3oz
110g	4oz
125g	$4^1/2$oz
150g	5oz
175g	6oz
200g	7oz
225g	8oz
250g	9oz
275g	10oz
350g	12oz
400g	14oz
450g	1lb
700g	$1^1/2$lb
900g	2lb
1.3kg	3lb
1.8kg	4lb
2.3kg	5lb

measurements

millimetres	inches
3mm	$^1/8$ inch
5mm	$^1/4$ inch
1cm	$^1/2$ inch
2cm	$^3/4$ inch
2.5cm	1 inch
3cm	$1^1/4$ inches
4cm	$1^1/2$ inches
4.5cm	$1^3/4$ inches
5cm	2 inches
7.5cm	3 inches
10cm	4 inches
13cm	5 inches
15cm	6 inches
18cm	7 inches
20cm	8 inches
23cm	9 inches
25cm	10 inches
28cm	11 inches
30cm	12 inches

I have always been drawn to recipes that make the most of a few simple ingredients, letting their wonderful natural flavours, aromas and goodness shine through. For me this ethos is perfectly summed up by the rustic simplicity and healthy, hearty diet of the Mediterranean, with fragrant focaccias and honey-drenched breads, crisp salads and savoury tarts, hearty soups and stews, oil-rich fish and crunchy vegetables, and desserts bursting with cherries, plums and figs. *A Taste of Sunshine* is a recollection of some of the finest cuisine I have tasted on my travels over the past year – my souvenirs from sunnier climes if you like – and I hope they remind you of happy summer holidays too.

The health-giving properties of a Mediterranean lifestyle are now widely accepted, and while *A Taste of Sunshine* is not strictly a diet book, the recipes can form part of a healthier, happier lifestyle. Nothing is restricted or banished. The emphasis is instead on variety and abundance and simple, natural ingredients – ripe, pungent cheeses, golden honey, sunshine oranges and lemons, fiery chillies, juicy tomatoes, fragrant basil, freshly pressed olive oil. Of course, to be truly Continental, and to get the best out of your food, I believe you should always use the freshest possible ingredients. I have adapted many of the recipes in *A Taste of Sunshine* to reflect what is available locally, creating a wonderful marriage of cultures and foods. The classic French tarte Tatin is packed with Bramley apples, while that Irish staple, soda bread, is made with olive oil.

I hope as you delve further into this book, and grow more confident in your cookery skills, you will experiment more with the recipes and ingredients suggested – after all, mixing and matching is part of the casual Mediterranean attitude to cooking and eating. Why not try grilled sardines as part of a leisurely weekend breakfast, or brioche, as the French do, served as a dessert, perhaps even stuffed with a generous scoop of toffee apple ice cream or slowly melting semifreddo? You can also make a meal out of any snack – simply serve with a salad and home-baked bread.

The recipes in *A Taste of Sunshine* do not require long hours slaving over a hot stove. Some recipes, such as the peppered steak with Béarnaise sauce or the country omelette, can be made in minutes. Others, such as the stews and casseroles, need a little preparation, but then they can be left in the oven to basically cook themselves. And, of course, many of the salads and desserts require no cooking at all. All of which leaves you lots of time to sit back, relax, and enjoy a nice glass of wine!

Jenny Bristow

change to a mediterranean lifestyle

The people of the Mediterranean have one of the healthiest diets I know; they live longer, suffer less from heart disease and certain types of cancer, and have a lower rate of obesity. Yet theirs is not a diet obsessed with counting calories or banishing whole food groups. Their attitude to cooking and eating is simple, casual and relaxed, and their meals are packed full of goodness and variety.

The primary source of dietary fat in the Mediterranean is olive oil, which is rich in antioxidants and essential vitamins. Fresh, local fruit and vegetables are eaten in abundance, while dairy products are eaten little but often. Fish and poultry are often favoured over red meat, and no meal would be complete without a glass of wine, now widely known to reduce cholesterol. Garlic and herbs are often used instead of salt, and honey instead of sugar.

Meals regularly consist of three courses, eaten leisurely and late, preferably outside, but certainly in good company. The people of the Mediterranean allow time to savour and digest food, and for the body to recognise that its hunger has been sated. I was both surprised and impressed when dining late into the evening in the south of France to be asked by the restaurateur if the ladies would like a shawl to keep them warm – he kept a stock of shawls just for this purpose.

In the UK and Ireland the average time it takes to prepare and cook a family meal is fifteen minutes. And as cooking times have become shorter, portion sizes have increased dramatically – super-sized, deep-filled ready-meals are zapped in the microwave and hastily consumed in front of the television with little by way of conversation or interaction. We have, it seems in some cases, forgotten not only the art of cooking, but the art of eating.

One reason I believe the Mediterranean diet is so healthy is because all meals are cooked fresh from raw, unprocessed ingredients. Indeed, preparation for meals often starts at the local market, where produce is prodded, tested and tasted prior to purchase – only the very best makes it into the shopping basket. I was initially bemused to be asked one morning in the market on what day I intended to eat the Brie I had selected. I was then presented with a wedge of cheese that would be exactly ripe on the day of consumption.

The Mediterranean diet is not, however, a strict regime. Much has been made recently of the claim that 'French women don't diet', and yet they enjoy all the naughty things in life – exquisite desserts, luscious pastries, thick custards and rich creams. Even chocolate is considered an essential part of the diet, as long as it is consumed in moderation, is of good quality and has a high cocoa content. So a little bit of what you fancy really does do you good!

Living a healthier lifestyle is not just about what we eat, but about how we eat. The recipes in this book are designed to let you cook and eat, live and relax, and experience a little of the Mediterranean lifestyle around your table, at any time of the year. So go on, bring a little sunshine into your life today.

essential ingredients

There are some ingredients you should always keep in your larder or fridge – flour, eggs, butter, milk, cheese, herbs, oil, vinegar … From these few simple ingredients, you can make any number of wholesome, satisfying meals, such as quiche or cheese soufflé.

Fruit and vegetables should be bought fresh and used as soon as possible to ensure you get all the goodness out of them. Bread should also be bought or made and consumed within two days.

honey

Honey really is sunshine in a jar! It can be added to nearly any dish as a natural sweetener and has fewer calories and carbohydrates than sugar. The flavour of the honey is determined by the blossoms visited by the bees, and there are simply hundreds of varieties to choose from. My favourites are lavender, orange-blossom, chestnut, rosemary and heather, but you can also buy such unusual flavours as avocado, blueberry and eucalyptus. Generally, the darker the honey, the stronger the flavour. Runny honey is best for cooking, simply because its texture is easier to work with.

mustard

Mustard should be used as a cooking ingredient as well as a condiment as it adds lots of flavour to food, with few calories and very little fat. Dijon mustard, from Burgundy in eastern France, is the most famous and, I think, the most flavoursome.

garlic

Garlic has many health-giving properties – it is said to ward off colds and lower blood pressure. It is a great way to flavour food without adding salt.

olives

It would be impossible not to mention olives, a staple of the Mediterranean, in this cookbook! Large, small, stuffed, skewered, pressed, sweet or salty – there are so many different ways to eat olives – and that is even before you start cooking with them!

Green olives are picked while unripe, which makes them denser and more bitter than brown or black olives, which stay on the tree until fully ripened. Olives become bitter if they are cooked too long, so always add them to hot dishes at the last minute.

olive oil

The flavour of olive oil is influenced by the variety of olive, the soil and climate. It is the most perfumed type of oil and should not be used unless you want some of the flavour to come through. Extra virgin olive oil comes from the first pressing of the olives and no other oils are blended with it. Use extra virgin olive oil in dressings, but just olive oil (not virgin) for cooking as it can cope with slightly higher temperatures.

The health benefits of olives and olive oil are now well documented, and they are believed to be one of the reasons the people of the Mediterranean lead longer, healthier lives. Rich in vitamins A, D, E and K and other antioxidants, an olive-rich diet can help prevent heart disease, lower cholesterol and blood pressure, and help delay the signs of ageing. Try to eat a little every day, whether you splash it over a salad or pasta dish or replace your usual cooking oil entirely.

vinegar

Not just for fish and chips, vinegar comes in many flavours and colours, and I have used a wide variety in this book. Buy the best you can afford as some cheaper vinegars are too acidic and lacking in flavour.

Wine vinegar is made from soured wine and has a distinctive sweet-sharp flavour. Red wine vinegar is great for adding a hint of colour to vinaigrettes and marinades. But my absolute favourite – and the most versatile – is balsamic vinegar. Usually made from red grapes, it has a distinctive sweet–sour fruity aroma and is a great addition to both sweet and savoury dishes. Add a splash to red meat to tenderise the cut, use a dash to bring out the flavour of strawberries and tomatoes, or mix into potato salad. You can also try varying the type and make of balsamic used – it comes in various shades, from a dark, syrupy brown to white. The price of balsamic vinegar varies greatly – look for the word 'tradizionale' or the place of origin, Modena in Italy. 'Aceto balsemico' is the cheaper variety, matured for a much shorter length of time, and often containing added sugar.

You could also experiment with raspberry, cider, rice wine and sherry vinegar.

essential ingredients

cheese

Cheese is a great source of calcium and some varieties are surprisingly low in fat. It is worth experimenting with unusual cheeses, especially on a cheese board, but many become rubbery when cooked for too long or at too high a temperature. Heat-tolerant cheeses such as mozzarella and Emmenthal are best for novice cooks.

Store cheese near the bottom of the refrigerator, where temperature fluctuations are minimal. If the cheese has been cut, wrap it tightly in plastic to hold in the moisture. If it hasn't been cut, wrap it first in waxed paper, then with plastic wrap to allow the cheese to breathe.

Mozzarella is a soft, round, white cheese traditionally made from the milk of the water buffalo. Most people know mozzarella as a pizza topping – it takes on a lovely stringy texture when heated – but it is widely used in salads and pasta dishes.

Mascarpone is often described as a curd cheese, although it is actually more similar to yoghurt. Soft and creamy, it has a slightly sweet flavour and is often used in desserts.

Feta is a crumbly Greek cheese made from sheep or goat's milk. It has a high salt content, so soak it in cold water or milk for a few minutes before use.

Parmesan is a very hard cheese from the Parma region of Italy. It is wonderful shaved over salads and pasta, or as a topping on bruschetta and pizza.

Ricotta is a moist, white cheese traditionally made from cow's milk. It is often used in lasagne.

Fontina is a dense, straw-coloured cheese from northern Italy. It has a delicate nutty flavour with a hint of honey that intensifies when cooked.

Emmenthal is a hard, holed cheese with a fruity flavour.

Gruyère is very similar to Emmenthal but with a denser texture.

Roquefort is known as the 'king of cheeses'. Its flavour combines the sweet caramel taste of sheep's milk with the sharp tang of blue mould.

Camembert is a famous French cheese with a creamy texture and delicate salty flavour. It is sold in distinctive round wooden containers.

herbs

It would be impossible to own all the herbs on earth, but a few basic ones will provide you with all you need, and a bit of variety too.

Dried herbs are a lot more potent than fresh herbs. You should use approximately 1 teaspoon of dried herbs for every tablespoonful of fresh herbs.

Basil is the main ingredient in pesto and is used widely in the south of France and Italy. Great raw or cooked, I think basil really enhances the flavour of tomatoes and tomato-based sauces.

Parsley is a much-used and loved herb, best added during the last few moments of cooking, sprinkled raw over salads, or used as a garnish. Italian flat-leaf parsley has a stronger flavour than its curly cousin but is also less bitter. Dried parsley has very little flavour and really isn't worth buying.

Oregano is a warm and slightly bitter herb, mostly used in Greek and Italian cooking with tomato sauces, fried vegetables and grilled meat. **Marjoram** has a milder and slightly sweeter flavour than oregano, with unusual pine and citrus overtones.

spices

Spices will have better flavour and a longer shelf life if you buy them whole – as berries, seeds, pods or quills – and grind them just before use.

Saffron threads are carefully cultivated from the saffron crocus flower and are very expensive to buy. Luckily, a little goes a long way. Contrary to popular belief, the threads should be vivid red, not yellow, in colour.

Nutmeg can be bought ready-ground, but it quickly loses a lot of its flavour, and I find it best to buy the whole seed and grate it as and when necessary. **Mace** is made from the same spice plant, this time the hard outer casing of the seed. It has a similar taste to nutmeg, though slightly more bitter. It is impossible to grind at home and should be bought powdered.

Star anise cloves are contained in beautiful star-shaped pods. They have a strong liquorice flavour – a little goes a long way.

Cardamom is an important curry spice, but it can also be used in baking and is wonderful with citrus fruits.

cooking with wine

Wine is often used in cooking to enhance and intensify the flavour of food. There are many guides to choosing the right wine to accompany a meal, but I think your own personal taste should dictate, so cook only with a wine you would actually drink. It does not have to be an expensive vintage, but I would avoid using bottles labelled 'cooking wine' as they tend to have a very high salt content. The process of heating and reducing the wine will only make it more acidic and vinegary. Another simple but effective idea is to use wine from the same region as your cuisine. For example, I would use a full-bodied red from the Rhone Valley in the south of France with the recipe for boeuf en daube.

Generally, cook the wine slowly and do not let it boil as it will impair the flavour. It is a good idea to serve the same wine with dinner as the one you cooked with. If you have a little of the bottle left over, I find it very handy to freeze the wine in ice-cube trays for future cooking use.

red wine

Red wine is rich in antioxidants that lower cholesterol and help prevent heart disease. Generally, Merlot and Pinot Noir are good all-rounders, while Cabernet Sauvignon and Syrah/Shiraz are robust, full-bodied wines that make good rich sauces and marinades.

white wine

Dry or medium-dry white wines, such as Sauvignon Blanc and Chardonnay, make an excellent addition to creamy sauces and a good accompaniment to any fish, seafood or white meat recipe. Sweeter, fruitier white wines, such as Riesling and Semillon, and dessert wines such as Muscat de Beaumes de Venise, should be used in desserts only.

rosé wine

Many wine connoisseurs frown upon rosé wine, and you can't cook with it, but it is very popular in Provence and the Loire Valley. I like rosé served very cold with a light meal in warm weather.

wine substitutes

If you don't want to use wine in your cooking, there are plenty of wine substitutes available, including non-alcoholic wines. Cranberry juice or even a dash of balsamic vinegar can be used as a substitute for red wine. White grape juice or apple juice can be used as a substitute for white wine.

liqueurs, brandies and fortified wines

Marsala is a sweet, fortified wine similar in texture and colour to port. It is very popular in Italy and is mostly used with chicken and in desserts.

Calvados is a brandy with a delicate apple flavour. It is mostly used in sauces and desserts.

Amaretto is a thick, brandy-based liqueur with the concentrated flavour of almonds. It works very well with chocolate, coffee and fruit.

Fruit juice makes an excellent substitute for liqueurs, brandies and fortified wines.

breads

There is nothing more **welcoming** than the **aroma** of freshly baked bread. Serve **warm** and **thickly sliced**, spread with homemade jam or topped with **cheese and chutney**. Perfect for breakfast, lunch and dinner.

A soft, light Italian bread best served straight from the oven and drizzled with a little olive oil.

sundried tomato
and black olive
focaccia

Focaccia can be left plain or flavoured with a variety of different ingredients such as olives, herbs or pine nuts. Here I have added some sundried tomatoes for a little extra sweetness and a burst of colour.

Mix the yeast, sugar and water in a large bowl and leave for 4–5 minutes to allow the yeast to activate. Add the flour, salt and 2 dsp of olive oil. Mix well to form a soft dough, then turn out onto a lightly floured, cool surface and knead for approximately 8–10 minutes. Lightly brush a large bowl with the remaining olive oil. Place the dough in the bowl, cover with clingfilm and leave in a warm place for $1^1/2$–$1^3/4$ hours until the dough has risen and doubled in size.

10g/^{1}/2oz dried yeast
25g/1oz caster sugar
275ml/^{1}/2pt warm water
450g/1lb plain flour – sieved
^{1}/2 tsp salt
3 dsp olive oil

Turn the dough out onto a lightly floured, cool worktop and knead again for 3–4 minutes. Carefully fold in the olives and sundried tomatoes. Additional ingredients such as herbs or pine nuts can also be added at this stage. Shape the bread into a flat round approximately 4cm/1^1/2 inches thick. Sprinkle the olive oil over the top of the bread, cover with clingfilm again and set aside in a warm place for a further 40–50 minutes until the dough has doubled in size again. Remove the clingfilm and place on a baking sheet. Bake in the oven @ 200°C/gas mark 6 for approximately 30 minutes until the bread is golden and crusty.

Serve warm.

225g/8oz black olives – pitted
110g/4oz sundried tomatoes – sliced
1 dsp olive oil

16

Soda bread is traditionally Irish, but here I have added a little olive oil to give it the flavour of the Mediterranean. Delicious served fresh from the oven, soda bread can also make a great pizza base.

flat olive oil
soda bread

serves 4–6

Sieve the flour, bicarbonate of soda and salt into a bowl, then add the bran and oatmeal. Mix 3 dsp of olive oil together with the wheat germ oil and add to the flour along with the buttermilk. Mix to form a stiff but slightly sticky dough.

Turn the dough out onto a lightly floured surface and knead gently to remove any cracks. Divide the dough into two, shape into rounds and flatten. Using a sharp knife, make a few slashes diagonally across the top of the rounds. Brush with the remaining olive oil before placing the rounds on a lightly floured baking sheet. Bake in the oven @ 220°C/gas mark 7 for 15–20 minutes. When cooked through, the bread will be firm, golden and sound hollow when tapped on the base. Wrap in a clean, dry tea towel and allow to cool before serving.

Serve topped with soft cheese and the melon jam on page 23 or as an accompaniment to stews and casseroles, such as the roasted pork and bean stew on page 87.

75g/3oz soda bread flour
110g/4oz wholemeal flour
1 tsp bicarbonate of soda
1/2 tsp salt
25g/1oz bran
25g/1oz oatmeal
4 dsp olive oil
1 tsp wheat germ oil – optional
275ml/1/2pt buttermilk – approximately

If you prefer white to brown bread, simply replace the wholemeal flour with 150g/5oz of self-raising soda bread flour. If soda bread flour is unavailable, use strong flour instead.

The dough for this bread needs to be prepared the day before, but the bread is best eaten warm and straight from the oven.

warm spiced
honey
bread

Honey can be used to sweeten bread instead of sugar, and the flavour of the bread will be influenced by the type of honey you choose.

Clover, thyme, orange-blossom, even dandelion and eucalyptus – there are simply hundreds of varieties of honey to choose from.

Place the flour, nutmeg, ginger, salt and bicarbonate of soda in a large bowl. Mix in the milk and honey, adding both at the same time. This will require quite a lot of mixing because the honey is very sticky. Finally, add the olive oil and mix again. The dough should be quite runny and have a sticky texture.

Wrap the dough in clingfilm and place in the fridge for 12 hours.

Line a shallow rectangular baking tin, approximately 15cm/6 inches by 25cm/10 inches, with greaseproof paper. Remove the dough from the fridge and place it in the tin. Bake in the oven for 45–50 minutes @ 200°C/gas mark 6.

Place the lemon zest and honey in a small saucepan. Mix well and heat through until hot and bubbling.

Remove the bread from the oven and drizzle the warm honey and lemon syrup over the top.

Serve immediately.

450g/1lb plain flour – sieved
1 tsp nutmeg – grated
1 tsp dried ginger
pinch salt
1 tsp bicarbonate of soda
275ml/^{1}/2pt milk
450g/1lb honey – runny or very soft
1 dsp olive oil

zest of 1 lemon
4 dsp heather or lavender honey

Crêpes can be filled with all kinds of ingredients, sweet or savoury, or served simply with a sprinkling of lemon juice and sugar. I really love this combination of apples and maple syrup – perfect for breakfast.

crêpes
with apple
and maple syrup

serves 4–6

Whisk the flour, egg, milk, butter and salt in a large bowl until smooth and creamy. Transfer the batter to a jug, cover with clingfilm and place in the fridge for at least 30 minutes.

Heat a non-stick frying pan and brush with a little melted butter. Pour over sufficient batter to cover the base of the pan, then tilt the pan until the bottom is evenly coated. As the batter cooks, bubbles will form on its surface. Cook the crêpe for approximately 1–2 minutes until these bubbles burst, then flip it over and cook for 1 minute more. Turn the crêpe out onto a baking sheet, cover and place in the oven @ 150°C/gas mark 2 to keep warm. Continue making the remainder of the crêpes in the same way, brushing the pan with a little butter each time.

75g/3oz plain flour
1 egg – lightly beaten
275ml/¹/2pt milk
25g/1oz butter – melted
pinch salt

Place the apples, sugar, butter and lemon juice in a saucepan and simmer gently until the apples have softened but are still holding their shape. Remove from the heat and set to one side to cool slightly.

Spoon a little of the cooked apple in a line across the centre of each crêpe. Fold over the edges and roll. Serve immediately drizzled with maple syrup.

450g/1lb apples – peeled, cored and cut into wedges
50g/2oz soft brown sugar
1 tbsp butter
1 tbsp lemon juice
4 dsp maple syrup

According to one legend, this crêpe dish was invented in Monaco in 1895 when a waiter accidentally set fire to the sauce. It was then served to Prince Edward of Wales, the future king of England, who named it after his companion's young daughter, Suzette.

crêpes
suzettes

serves 4

crêpes

Make the crêpes using the recipe opposite.

orange butter

Mix the lemon zest, orange zest, orange juice and icing sugar in a bowl. Add the butter and mix well to form a paste. Place the orange butter in the fridge and leave to chill for 15–20 minutes.

zest of 1 lemon
zest of 1 orange
2 tbsp freshly squeezed orange juice
2 tbsp icing sugar
50g/2oz butter – softened

suzette sauce

Heat the butter in a frying pan. Add the sugar and cook until it just begins to brown. Add the orange juice and simmer for approximately 2 minutes.

Remove the butter from the fridge and spread it over the crêpes. Fold the crêpes into quarters and add to the pan four at a time. Toss gently until well coated in the sauce, then sprinkle with the brandy and liqueur. You can flambé the crêpes at this stage: set light to the sauce and baste the crêpes until the flame dies out.

Using a slotted spoon, remove the crêpes from the pan and arrange on individual plates. Pour a little sauce over the crêpes and serve immediately.

50g/2oz butter
50g/2oz caster sugar
juice of 1 orange
2–4 tbsp brandy
2 tbsp Grand Marnier or Cointreau

I love to eat brioche still warm from the oven and spread with pear and ginger jam.

brioche

Mix the yeast, sugar and water in a bowl and leave for 4–5 minutes to allow the yeast to activate. Add the flour, salt and eggs to the bowl and beat for 8–10 minutes. An electric mixer can be used set at slow speed. Gradually add the butter and continue to beat until the mixture is smooth and well combined. Shape the dough into a round, cover with clingfilm and place in the fridge overnight.

Remove the dough from the fridge and turn it out onto a lightly floured surface. Knead lightly. Transfer the brioche to a loaf tin, approximately 25cm/10 inches by 15cm/6 inches. Alternatively, you can make this brioche in several smaller loaf tins. Brush the surface of the bread with the egg and place in the oven @ 170°C/gas mark 3 for 30–40 minutes.

Remove the brioche from the oven and allow to cool slightly before serving.

10g/^{1}/2oz dried yeast
25g/1oz caster sugar
4 dsp warm water
450g/1lb plain flour – sieved
pinch salt
4 eggs – lightly beaten
125g/4^1/2oz unsalted butter – softened

1 egg – lightly beaten

pear and ginger jam

Peel, core and dice the pears, then place them in a large saucepan with the ginger, lemon juice and water. Simmer gently for 8–10 minutes until the fruit shows signs of softening, then reduce the temperature to just below simmering point.

Spread the sugar on a baking tray and place in the oven @ 190°C/gas mark 5 for 10–12 minutes to remove any moisture. Remove the sugar from the oven and add it immediately to the fruit. Stir gently over a low heat until all the sugar has dissolved, then turn up the heat and boil rapidly for approximately 10 minutes. To test if the jam is ready, take it off the heat, spoon a little liquid onto a chilled saucer and let it cool for a few seconds. Push it with your finger – if the surface of the jam wrinkles, the setting point has been reached. If not, boil for a further 5 minutes and test again. Remove the pan from the heat and leave it to one side to cool slightly. Pour the jam into sterilised jars (see opposite page) and seal. The jam should keep for up to 6 months if stored in a cool, dark cupboard.

900g/2lb pears – ripe, firm and with no blemishes
2.5cm/1 inch fresh ginger – peeled and grated
50g/2oz preserved ginger – finely sliced
juice of 2 lemons
275ml/^{1}/2pt water
900g/2lb preserving sugar

Homemade jam is a treat at any time of year and this one is quite unusual. It is best made with a chunky texture. Try it spread on warm bread and topped with melting Brie.

melon
jam

Jams, preserves and chutneys should be stored in airtight jars and, ideally, the jars should be sealed. Jam pot covers are readily available in supermarkets and contain paper discs, cellophane seals and elastic bands.

makes approximately 1.8kg/4lbs

2 cantaloupe melons
700g/1 1/2 lb caster sugar
75ml/3floz water
zest and juice of 2 large lemons
2 dsp Marsala wine or Jerez sherry

Wash the jars in hot soapy water and rinse well. Then, to sterilise the jars, place them in an oven @ 190°C/gas mark 5 for 15–20 minutes. Cool the jars before filling with warm jam and cover immediately with a paper disc. Allow the jam to cool completely, cover with a cellophane seal and secure with an elastic band. For best results, store in a cool, dark cupboard.

Cut the melons in half and remove the seeds. Scoop out the soft centre, discard the rind, and cut the flesh into large chunks. The flesh can be chopped more finely for a smoother jam.

Spread the sugar on a baking tray and place in the oven @ 190°C/ gas mark 5 for 10–12 minutes to remove any moisture.

While the sugar is warming, place the melon and the water in a heavy-based saucepan, cover and simmer gently until the melon has softened. Cooking times will vary according to the ripeness of the melon but should take around 10 minutes.

Add the warm sugar, lemon and wine or sherry to the saucepan and stir until the sugar dissolves. Turn the temperature up and boil rapidly for 30–45 minutes. Do not over-boil or the jam will become a dark, unattractive colour. To test the setting point, follow the method given for the pear and ginger jam, opposite.

Remove the pan from the heat and leave to one side to cool slightly, then pour into sterilised jars and seal. The jam should keep for up to 6 months if stored in a cool, dark cupboard.

salads

Crisp, fresh and colourful, packed full of seasonal fruit and vegetables, **bursting** with **goodness** and **flavour**, salads really do capture the **essence of summer.** A great way to eat your greens.

Fresh, crisp and colourful, this bistro-style salad makes a delicious light lunch. It is also a great accompaniment to the sticky lemon chicken on page 82.

courgette and
french bean
salad

serves 4

dressing

Place all the ingredients except the mint in a blender and whiz until smooth. Next, add the mint and whiz lightly until well mixed but not completely blended. Pour the dressing into a bowl and place in the fridge to chill while preparing the salad.

2 hard-boiled egg yolks
125ml/4floz Greek yoghurt
125ml/4floz olive oil
juice of 1 lemon
1 tsp clear honey
1 dsp white wine vinegar
1 clove garlic – peeled and crushed
8–10 leaves mint – chopped

salad

Place the beans and courgettes in boiling salted water, cover and simmer for no more than 1–2 minutes. Drain and refresh the beans and courgettes by quickly plunging them into cold water. Pat dry.

Mix together the beans, courgettes, apple, avocado and lemon juice in a large bowl. Drizzle with the dressing and toss lightly.

To serve the dish, arrange the chicory leaves on a large serving platter. Scatter with the beans, courgette, apple and avocado and drizzle with a little more dressing. Serve slightly warm, garnished with fresh mint.

1 green apple – peeled, cored and diced
1 avocado – peeled, stoned and diced
juice of 1 lemon
340g/12oz courgettes – cut into fine strips or grated
12 French beans – trimmed and halved
2 heads chicory
small handful of mint

Bittersweet citrus fruits make an unusual and refreshing addition to any salad. This one works really well with crusty brown bread or as an accompaniment to game birds such as duck.

honeyed citrus salad

serves 4

dressing

Pour the red wine vinegar, olive oil and honey into a screw-top jar. Tightly secure the lid and shake well. Set to one side to allow the flavours to develop while preparing the salad.

1 dsp red wine vinegar
1 dsp olive oil
2 dsp orange-blossom honey

Try varying the types of citrus fruit used – ugli fruit, for example, make an interesting addition.

salad

Place the pine nuts on a baking tray and toast in the oven @ 170°C/gas mark 3 for 10–15 minutes until golden brown. Remove from the oven and leave to one side to cool.

110g/4oz pine nuts

Using a sharp knife, peel the oranges and grapefruit, remove the pith and cut into segments. Mix the fruit and arrange on a large, shallow serving platter. Scatter the celery over the fruit and arrange the rocket leaves around the outside of the platter.

2 oranges
2 blood oranges
2 grapefruit
1 small stalk celery – cut into matchsticks
good handful fresh rocket
pinch salt
pinch freshly ground black pepper

Approximately 5 minutes before serving, lightly drizzle the dressing over the salad. Season well with salt and pepper and scatter with the toasted pine nuts.

This dish is very simple to prepare but full of strong, rich flavours and hearty enough to be served as a main course.

salad of
mozzarella
and
sundried tomato
with serrano ham and chorizo

serves 4–6

Serrano ham originates from Spain and means 'from the mountains', where it is traditionally dried and cured in the open air. Chorizo also comes from Spain and is made of pork, sweet paprika and garlic. Both meats are now readily available in supermarkets.

Arrange the chorizo and half the mozzarella on a serving platter and scatter with basil. Layer with serrano ham and top with the olives and sundried tomatoes. Arrange the lettuce around the edges of the platter and drizzle the entire salad with olive oil. Season well with pepper and finally top with the remaining mozzarella.

Serve the salad with fresh crusty bread and a little extra olive oil on the side.

110g/4oz chorizo – thickly sliced
150g/5oz buffalo mozzarella – finely sliced
good handful basil leaves – roughly chopped
225g/8oz serrano ham – cut into strips
12 mixed black and green olives – pitted
6–8 sundried tomatoes in oil – finely sliced
small handful oak-leaf lettuce
small handful assorted lettuce
2–3 dsp extra virgin olive oil
pinch freshly ground black pepper

This simple salad is full of texture and flavour.
I love the sharp sweetness of the balsamic vinegar
combined with the onion.

crispy trio of
onion salad

serves 3–4

Heat the olive oil and the butter in a large frying pan until hot and sizzling. Add the sugar, onion and red onion, and cook until the onions are crispy and have started to blacken. Turn the heat down, add the spring onions and balsamic vinegar and cook for a further 1–2 minutes until everything has warmed through.

Remove the pan from the heat and leave to one side to cool slightly. Arrange the radicchio on individual plates and top with the onions. Pour over any remaining juices and serve warm.

2 tbsp extra virgin olive oil
25g/1oz butter
1 tbsp brown sugar
1 onion – coarsely sliced
1 red onion – coarsely sliced
1 bunch spring onions – chopped
2 tbsp balsamic vinegar
1/2 head radicchio

A quick and easy pasta salad that can be served
warm or cold.

pasta
with rocket and walnuts

serves 4

Cook the pasta in boiling salted water. Cooking time will depend on the kind of pasta you use – follow the instructions on the packet.

In a separate pan heat the olive oil, balsamic vinegar, walnuts and spring onions for 2–3 minutes. Do not overcook, as this will spoil the colour of the spring onions.

Drain the pasta and place in a large bowl. Add the cheese to the warm pasta and drizzle with the walnut and spring onion dressing. Toss lightly. Just before serving, add the rocket leaves or flat-leaf parsley and toss again.

225g/8oz pasta – fresh or dried
    tagliatelle or penne
1 dsp olive oil
1 dsp balsamic vinegar
50g/2oz walnuts – coarsely
    chopped
2–3 spring onions – coarsely
    chopped
110g/4oz Irish Ballyblue cheese –
    diced
small bunch rocket leaves or
    flat-leaf parsley

This salad originates from Nice in the south of France and comes in many different versions. I love the combination of warm baby potatoes and fresh vegetables tossed in a tasty vinaigrette dressing.

salade niçoise

serves 3–4

vinaigrette

Mix the shallot, olive oil, vinegar, lemon juice, honey, seasoning and mustard in a screw-top jar. Shake well, add the caster sugar and shake again. Chill the dressing in the fridge until ready to serve.

1 shallot – finely chopped
4 tbsp extra virgin olive oil
3 tbsp white wine vinegar
juice of 1/2 lemon
2 tsp runny honey
pinch sea salt
pinch freshly ground black pepper
1 tsp Dijon mustard
1 tsp caster sugar

salade niçoise

Boil the potatoes in a large saucepan of salted water for approximately 8–10 minutes or until tender. Drain, brush with olive oil and black pepper and grill for 2–3 minutes. Set to one side.

10–12 baby potatoes – halved
2 dsp olive oil
pinch freshly ground black pepper

Plunge the green beans into a saucepan of boiling water and cook for 2 minutes. Drain the beans and refresh under cold water.

110g/4oz fine green beans – trimmed and halved

Season the tuna steaks with salt and black pepper and sprinkle with balsamic vinegar. Lightly oil a grill pan or frying pan and heat to a high temperature. Add the tuna to the pan and cook for 3–4 minutes on each side or as desired. Like steak, tuna can be eaten rare, medium or well done. When cooked, remove the tuna from the pan and flake into large chunks using a fork.

2 tuna steaks – 110–150g/4–5oz each
pinch sea salt
pinch freshly ground black pepper
2 dsp balsamic vinegar

Mix the potatoes, beans, olives, tomatoes and 4 tbsp of vinaigrette in a bowl. Assemble the lettuce on a plate and scatter with the vegetables and tuna chunks. Garnish with strips of anchovy and sprinkle with lemon juice, sea salt and black pepper.

10–12 black olives – pitted
225g/8oz cherry tomatoes – halved
assorted lettuce leaves
2–4 anchovies – cut into strips
1 lemon – juice
pinch sea salt
pinch freshly ground black pepper

This salad can be eaten cold, but I like it served with the tuna and potatoes still a little warm.

Chèvre chaud is a classic French snack. Here I have drizzled the cheese with honey before flashing it under a hot grill.

warm goat's cheese salad
with watercress pesto

serves 4

Crottin du Chavignol are small flat discs of goat's cheese from the Berry and Périgord regions of France. They are the perfect size and shape for toasting on sliced baguette. Alternatively, bûche- or log-shaped chèvres can also be used.

watercress pesto

Place the watercress, garlic and nuts in a blender and whiz until smooth. Add the olive oil and whiz again to form a thick sauce. Next, add the Parmesan and season with a little salt and pepper to taste. Whiz again. If the pesto is too thick, add a little more olive oil.

110g/4oz fresh watercress
1 clove garlic
25g/1oz walnuts and/or pine nuts
125ml/4floz olive oil
50g/2oz Parmesan
pinch salt
pinch freshly ground black pepper

goat's cheese salad

Brush the bread with the oil and a little of the pesto. Slice the goat's cheese to fit the bread, cut approximately 2.5cm/1 inch thick. Arrange the cheese on top of the bread and drizzle with honey. Place on a baking tray below a hot grill until the cheese is golden and bubbling.

4 slices baguette or toasted bread
2 dsp extra virgin olive oil
300g/11oz goat's cheese
2 dsp runny honey

Remove the bread from the grill and arrange on a plate. Drizzle a little more pesto around the bread and top with the salad leaves. Sprinkle with the walnuts and serve warm as a starter or light lunch.

1 packet mixed green salad leaves
25g/1oz walnuts

A light and simple salad, ideal for a quick snack or lunch.

mozzarella
salad
with celery, pear and apple

Make a vinaigrette dressing by mixing the olive oil, vinegar and mustard in a small bowl or by placing the ingredients in a screw-top jar and shaking well.

2 dsp extra virgin olive oil
1 dsp white wine vinegar
1/2 tsp Dijon mustard

In a separate bowl, mix the celery, apple and pear. Add the basil and mozzarella and mix again. Pour the dressing over the salad, toss well and serve.

4 stalks celery – chopped
2 apples – peeled, cored and diced
4 pears – peeled, cored and diced
2 dsp basil – coarsely chopped
110g/4oz mozzarella – cut into fine strips

34

summer
COUSCOUS

Place the saffron threads in the warm water and set to one side to infuse for 10 minutes.

Melt the butter in a large saucepan pan and add the couscous, hot water and orange juice. Stir well to coat the couscous, then turn the heat off and set to one side for approximately 10 minutes until the couscous has absorbed the liquid and the mixture has doubled in size.

Add the saffron and its liquid, orange zest, sultanas, cumin, nuts, olive oil and pepper to the couscous and mix well. Serve warm or cold, garnished with sprigs of coriander.

10–12 saffron threads
6 dsp warm water

25g/1oz butter
175g/6oz couscous
275ml/1/2pt hot water
zest and juice of 1 orange
125g/41/2oz sultanas
1/2 tsp cumin powder
110g/4oz pistachio nuts – shelled and toasted
110g/4oz flaked almonds – toasted
3 dsp extra virgin olive oil
good pinch freshly ground black pepper
sprigs of coriander to serve

This is a lovely, light salad, combining fruit, nuts and spices. I like to serve it with the grilled chops and apricot and orange sauce on page 84.

baked
COUSCOUS
pilaf

Arrange the pine nuts on a baking tray and toast in the oven @ 170°C/gas mark 3 for 10–15 minutes until golden brown.

Place the couscous in a large bowl and pour over the hot stock. Leave to one side for approximately 10 minutes to let the flavours infuse and until the couscous has absorbed the liquid and has doubled in size.

Heat the olive oil in a frying pan and lightly cook the onion for 1–2 minutes until slightly softened. Remove the onion from the pan and add to the couscous. Next add the pine nuts, chilli, coriander seeds, parsley and feta and mix well. Transfer the mixture to a round, ovenproof dish and bake in the oven @ 200°C/gas mark 6 for 10–15 minutes.

Remove the couscous from the oven and serve with the poulet basquaise on page 83 or, for a light lunch, top with a little of the tapenade on page 55.

50g/2oz pine nuts

225g/8oz couscous
150ml/1/4pt chicken or vegetable stock

2 dsp olive oil
1 red onion – finely diced
1 green chilli – deseeded and finely chopped
1 tsp coriander seeds – crushed
1 dsp flat-leaf parsley – coarsely chopped
110g/4oz feta cheese – crumbled

Couscous is a wonderful ingredient that quickly and easily absorbs other flavours. In this recipe I love the contrast between the fiery chilli and creamy feta.

This unusual salad is just bursting with fresh, crisp flavours and textures. A perfect accompaniment to any grilled or barbecued food.

mixed salad
with caramelised apples, fennel and nuts

serves 4–6

For many centuries fennel has been a popular medicinal and culinary herb. It has a sweet aniseed flavour, which can be used to enhance sauces and marinades. The thick stalks of Florence fennel can also be eaten as a vegetable.

dressing

Place the olive oil, balsamic vinegar and chilli in a bowl or in a screw-top jar and stir or shake vigorously for 30 seconds.

6 tbsp extra virgin olive oil
2 tbsp balsamic vinegar
1/2 red chilli – deseeded and chopped

salad

Place the walnuts and the pine nuts on a baking tray and roast in the oven at 170°C/gas mark 3 for 10–15 minutes to intensify their flavour.

50g/2oz walnuts
50g/2oz pine nuts
10g/1/2oz butter
2 green apples – unpeeled, cored and diced
1 dsp balsamic vinegar

Melt the butter in a griddle pan. Add the apples and cook for approximately 2–3 minutes until golden and caramelised. Sprinkle with a little balsamic vinegar during cooking.

Remove the fronds from the fennel and set to one side. Cut the bulb into matchsticks. Steam gently for 2–3 minutes, then set to one side to cool.

1 head Florence fennel

Mix the radicchio, rocket and oak-leaf lettuce and arrange on a large platter. Scatter with the fennel, caramelised apples and toasted nuts and drizzle with the dressing. Garnish with shavings of Parmesan and fronds of fennel.

6–8 leaves radicchio – torn
small bunch rocket
small bunch oak-leaf lettuce
50g/2oz Parmesan – shaved

Serve immediately.

tarts

Rustic, hearty and healthy, these tarts are packed full of simple, wholesome ingredients — creamy cheeses, fresh, fragrant herbs, plump tomatoes, juicy olives ... Great for dinner parties, lunches and picnics.

Today's fashionable pies and tarts come stuffed with vegetables, herbs and cheese, but this is a very simple, traditional quiche, and one that has stood the test of time.

quiche **lorraine**

serves 6–8

Place the flour on a cool worktop. Make a well in the centre and add the oil, salt and butter. Gradually incorporate the flour. Next, add the water a little at a time until the mixture binds together. Knead well to form a soft dough. Wrap in clingfilm and place in the fridge for 15–30 minutes to allow the pastry to rest.

250g/9oz plain flour – sieved
2 dsp groundnut oil
pinch salt
150g/5oz butter or margarine – softened
3–4 dsp cold water

Remove the pastry from the fridge and place on a floured surface. Roll out to fit a lightly greased, shallow tin, approximately 23–25cm/9–10 inches in diameter. Line the tin with the pastry, pressing well into the sides. Trim off any excess pastry and prick the base lightly with a fork, then cover with a layer of grease-proof paper and some dried beans or lentils to prevent it from rising in the centre. Place in the oven @ 190°C/gas mark 5 for 15–20 minutes. Take the pastry case out of the oven, remove the beans or lentils and greaseproof paper, and set to one side to cool before filling.

Break the eggs into a large bowl and beat well. Add the nutmeg, cream and yoghurt and mix. Add half the cheese and mix lightly.

3 eggs
pinch nutmeg
275ml/$\frac{1}{2}$pt double cream
4 dsp yoghurt
50g/2oz Gruyère – grated
225g/8oz streaky bacon – cut into pieces
1 onion – sliced
1 tbsp fresh mixed herbs, e.g. basil, oregano and parsley
pinch freshly ground black pepper

Cook the bacon in a frying pan until it starts to crisp up – there is no need to add oil. Add the onion and cook for approximately 4–5 minutes until softened. Finally, add the mixed herbs and seasoning and turn off the heat.

Place the pastry case on a baking sheet and scatter the bacon, onion and herbs over the base. Pour in the egg mixture and top with the remaining cheese. Cook in the oven @ 190°C/gas mark 5 for 20–25 minutes until firm, golden and slightly risen.

Serve hot or cold with a salad of mixed leaves and herbs.

A great tart made with crisp Parmesan pastry.
Ideal for lunch or as a starter.

asparagus, spinach and mushroom tart

serves 6–8

parmesan pastry

Place all the ingredients, except the water, in a food processor and whiz until they start to come together to form a dough. You may need to add a little water.

Roll out the pastry to line a lightly greased, loose-bottomed flan or quiche dish approximately 18cm/7 inches in diameter. Trim off any excess pastry from around the edges and cover with clingfilm. Place the dish in the fridge for 15–30 minutes to allow the pastry to rest. Remove the clingfilm and prick the base of the pastry case lightly with a fork. Cover with a layer of greaseproof paper and dried beans or lentils to prevent it rising in the centre. Bake @ 190°C/gas mark 5 for 10–15 minutes.

175g/6oz plain flour – sieved
50g/2 oz Parmesan
75g/3oz butter or margarine – softened
1 egg – lightly beaten
1–2 dsp cold water – optional

filling

Heat the butter or oil in a pan and add the mushrooms, then the asparagus and spinach. Heat gently for 2–3 minutes, then drain off the excess liquid and place in the baked pastry case. In a separate bowl, beat together the eggs, cream and yoghurt. Add the cheese and season. Pour the mixture into the pastry case and bake in the oven at 190°C/gas mark 5 for 20–25 minutes until the tart is cooked and well set. Garnish with parsley.

25g/1oz butter or 1 dsp olive oil
175g/6oz mushrooms – sliced
225g/8oz green asparagus – lightly steamed and cut into 2.5cm/1 inch pieces
110g/4oz spinach
3 eggs – lightly beaten
150ml/1/4pt double cream
2 dsp low fat yoghurt
75g/3oz cheddar or Parmesan – grated
pinch salt – optional
pinch freshly ground black pepper
small handful parsley – finely chopped

Pissaladière is basically a Provençal version of pizza, but the pastry is made with a lip to hold the filling.

pissaladière
with caramelised onions
olives and anchovies

serves 6–8

The base of this tart can be made with shortcrust pastry, bread or pizza dough, but for this recipe I have used a quick and easy no-roll buttermilk pastry, which also has a rather unique flavour.

Pissaladière can be eaten hot or cold and is an ideal picnic food. You can use whatever topping you like but I highly recommend this sweet and salty combination for a truly authentic experience.

buttermilk pastry

Place the flour, baking powder, cayenne pepper, Parmesan, buttermilk and oil in a large bowl and mix well to form a soft dough. Shape the dough into a round and place on a shallow rectangular baking tray approximately 25x30cm/10x12 inches. Flatten the dough to fit the tray, keeping a lip running around the edge of the tray. Allow the pastry to rest in the fridge for 15–30 minutes.

175g/6oz self-raising flour – sieved
1 tsp baking powder
1 tsp cayenne pepper
25g/1oz Parmesan – finely grated or shaved
275ml/1/2pt buttermilk
1 dsp sunflower oil

filling

Heat the butter and 2 dsp of olive oil in a large, shallow frying pan. Add the herbs, salt, pepper and onions and cook gently over a low heat for 1 hour. It is important that the onions do not brown but sauté slowly. Remove the pan from the heat and set the onions to one side to cool.

Remove the pastry from the fridge, brush with the remaining olive oil and cover with the onions. Arrange the anchovies and black olives over the onions in a lattice pattern and sprinkle with basil. Bake in the oven @ 220°C/gas mark 7 for 20–25 minutes until crisp and golden. Remove the pissaladière from the oven and scatter with a little more fresh basil. Cut into slices and serve warm.

25g/1oz butter
75ml/3floz extra virgin olive oil
good pinch dried herbs, e.g. thyme, basil or parsley
pinch salt – optional
pinch freshly ground black pepper
3 red onions – finely sliced
3 onions – finely sliced
6–8 anchovy fillets – halved lengthways
225g/8oz black olives – pitted and halved
small handful basil – torn

Ricotta is a traditional Italian soft cheese meaning 'cooked again'. Made from sheep's milk, it is naturally low in fat and salt, and its subtle flavour and creamy texture make it perfect for use in both sweet and savoury dishes.

tomato and
ricotta tart

serves 6

The easiest way to skin fresh tomatoes is to plunge them into boiling water for 20–25 seconds until the skin changes colour and wrinkles slightly. Then, using a sharp knife, gently peel the skin away from the flesh.

pastry

Place the flour, butter, egg, paprika, pepper and water in bowl or food processor and mix until all the ingredients come together to form a smooth dough. Turn out onto a cool, lightly floured worktop and knead to remove any cracks. Roll out to line a lightly greased, loose-bottomed flan dish, approximately 20–23cm/8–9 inches in diameter. Trim off any excess pastry, cover the dish with clingfilm and place in the fridge for 30 minutes. Remove the pastry case from the fridge, prick the base lightly with a fork and cover with greaseproof paper and a layer of dried beans or lentils to prevent it rising in the centre. Bake in the oven @ 190°C/gas mark 5 for 15–20 minutes. Remove from the oven, discard the beans or lentils and the greaseproof paper, and set to one side to cool.

225g/8oz plain flour – sieved
110g/4oz butter – softened
1 egg – lightly beaten
1/2 tsp paprika
pinch freshly ground black pepper
1 dsp cold water

filling

Place the ricotta, mustard, egg yolks and crème fraîche in a large bowl and mix well. Spread the mixture over the bottom of the baked pastry case and sprinkle with the basil. Arrange the sliced tomatoes in a circular pattern over the top of the tart. Sprinkle with salt, pepper and olive oil before baking in the oven @ 190°C/gas mark 5 for 20–30 minutes. Cooking time will depend upon the ripeness of the tomatoes – take care not to overcook.

Serve warm with a green, leafy salad.

500g/1lb 2oz ricotta
2 tsp Dijon mustard
2 egg yolks – lightly beaten
2 tbsp crème fraîche
1 dsp basil – finely chopped
6–8 tomatoes – skinned and finely sliced
pinch sea salt
pinch freshly ground black pepper
1 dsp extra virgin olive oil
good handful basil leaves – coarsely chopped

Fontina is a cow's milk cheese from the Aosta region of Italy. It has a distinctive, sweet taste, which combines wonderfully with the light smoky flavour of the salmon.

smoked salmon and fontina tart

serves 6

pastry

Place the flour, salt and pepper in a bowl. Rub in the butter until the mixture becomes crumbly. Add the egg and water and mix to a stiff but manageable dough. Roll out to a thickness of 1cm/1/2 inch and line a lightly buttered flan dish, approximately 18cm/7 inches in diameter. Trim off any excess pastry, cover the dish with clingfilm and place in the fridge for 15–30 minutes to rest. Remove the pastry case from the fridge and prick the base lightly with a fork. Cover with a layer of greaseproof paper and dried beans or lentils to prevent it rising in the centre and bake in the oven for 10 minutes @ 190°C/gas mark 5. Remove from the oven, discard the beans or lentils and the greaseproof paper, and set to one side to cool.

150g/6oz plain flour – sieved
pinch salt
pinch freshly ground black pepper
75g/3oz butter
1 egg – lightly beaten
1–2 dsp cold water

filling

Sprinkle the smoked salmon, chives and lemon zest over the base of the baked tart.

Make a cheese sauce by melting the butter in a saucepan, add the flour and mix well. Gradually add the milk, stirring constantly until the mixture begins to thicken. Remove the saucepan from the heat. Lightly beat the egg yolks and add them to the pan along with the cheese. Mix well, taste and season.

Beat the egg whites until they form stiff white peaks and carefully fold into the cheese sauce. Transfer the mixture to the pastry case and bake in the oven @ 200°C/gas mark 6 for 15 minutes until the topping is risen and golden. Serve garnished with lemon wedges and chives.

225g/8oz smoked salmon – chopped
1 dsp chives – finely chopped
zest of 1/2 lemon
25g/1oz butter
25g/1oz plain flour
275ml/1/2pt milk
2 eggs – separated
110g/4oz Fontina – roughly crumbled
pinch salt
pinch freshly ground black pepper
1 lemon – cut into wedges
small bunch chives – finely chopped

45

Simple, fresh and tasty, these tartlets make a lovely starter and are great for picnics.

parmesan and watercress
tartlets
with red onion marmalade

serves 6

tartlets

Place all the ingredients in a food processor and whiz until they bind together to form a soft dough. Roll out to the thickness of 1cm/^{1}/2 inch. Using a pastry cutter, cut into six rounds, approximately 10cm/4 inches in diameter. Line individual, lightly greased moulds or tins with the pastry and lightly prick each base with a fork. Cover with clingfilm and place in the fridge for 15–30 minutes. Remove from the fridge and cover with a layer of greaseproof paper and a layer of dried beans or lentils to prevent the pastry cases rising in the centre. Bake in the oven @ 190°C/gas mark 5 for 10 minutes. Remove from the oven, discard the beans or lentils and the greaseproof paper, and set to one side to cool.

225g/8oz flour – sieved
125g/4^1/2oz butter
1 egg – lightly beaten
2–3 dsp cold water

Melt the butter in a small frying pan. Add the onion and cook lightly for 1 minute. Add the watercress and remove the pan from the heat. Set to one side to cool.

25g/1oz butter
^{1}/2 small onion – finely sliced
small bunch watercress – lightly steamed
3 eggs – lightly beaten
275ml/^{1}/2pt double cream
110g/4oz Parmesan
^{1}/2 tsp paprika

Beat together the eggs and cream, then add the Parmesan, paprika, onion and watercress. Mix well. Pour the mixture into the pastry shells and bake in the oven @ 180°C/gas mark 4 for approximately 25 minutes until the tarts are golden and firm to the touch.

red onion marmalade

While the tarts are baking, make the red onion marmalade. Melt the butter in a saucepan and add the onion, water, vinegar and sugar. Cook for 12–15 minutes, stirring occasionally, until the mixture has reduced and the onions have softened. Season with black pepper to taste and set to one side to cool slightly.

25g/1oz butter
2 red onions – finely sliced
3–4 dsp water
4 dsp red wine vinegar
50g/2oz soft brown sugar
pinch freshly ground black pepper

Remove the tartlets from the moulds. Serve warm or cold, with a little red onion marmalade on the side.

snacks & soups

Light and **fluffy** cheese soufflé, fresh and **colourful** gazpacho, **rich spreads** and **chunky chutneys**. Great as **snacks**, starters or tapas, simply add salad and **fresh** bread for a real feast.

Quick, easy and colourful, this simple potato and vegetable omelette is Spanish in origin. Great on its own or served with a green salad for a tasty vegetarian meal.

country
omelette

serves 6

Heat the oil in a large frying pan. Add the peppers and tomatoes and cook gently for 2–3 minutes until softened. Next, add the potatoes in a circular pattern and cook for 10–12 minutes, turning occasionally, until they are a light golden brown in colour.

While the potatoes are cooking, beat together the eggs, milk, paprika and pepper in a large bowl. Pour the mixture into the frying pan containing the vegetables and cook until the omelette has set. You may need to tilt the mixture around the pan and finish it off under a hot grill to do this.

Slide the omelette onto a plate and serve hot or cold, garnished with fresh parsley.

1 dsp olive oil
1 red pepper – deseeded and diced
2 large ripe tomatoes – finely chopped
2 potatoes – peeled and finely sliced

4–5 eggs
2 tbsp milk
$1/2$ tsp paprika
good pinch freshly ground black pepper
1–2 dsp flat-leaf parsley – coarsely chopped

A classic Italian appetiser, bruschetta is simply thick slices of bread toasted lightly and rubbed with garlic.

warm parmesan
bruschetta
with grilled
mediterranean peppers

Place the peppers in a large bowl, add the honey and 1 dsp of olive oil and toss until the peppers are well coated. Cook the peppers under a hot grill until soft and slightly blackened.

Toast the bread under a hot grill until golden. Remove from the grill and rub both sides with garlic. Place the bread on a baking tray. Mix together the balsamic vinegar and the remainder of the olive oil and sprinkle over the toast.

Arrange the peppers on the bread and sprinkle with Parmesan, then pour over any remaining juices from the grilled peppers. Season with black pepper to taste.

Garnish with basil or a little of the pistou on page 68. Serve immediately.

2 yellow peppers – deseeded and cut into chunks
1 orange pepper – deseeded and cut into chunks
2 dsp runny honey
2 dsp extra virgin olive oil
2 thick slices bread
1 clove garlic – peeled and halved
2 dsp balsamic vinegar

110g/4oz Parmesan – shaved
pinch freshly ground black pepper

handful basil leaves – torn

Any type of bread will do, although the crunchier the better. Pain de campagne, baguette and ciabatta are ideal, while sourdough adds interest.

There are some wonderfully flavoured olive oils on the market, so why not try sprinkling the bruschetta with basil, chilli or lemon oil?

People worry about making soufflé, but this version is perfect for dinner parties. Most of the cooking is done the day before – just reheat when you are ready to serve.

twice-baked
cheese soufflé
with tarragon and paprika cream

serves 4

Prepare one large or 4 individual soufflé dishes by lightly greasing with a little melted butter. Sprinkle with a little cheddar, then place in the fridge to chill while you prepare the rest of the dish.

Heat the milk, spring onions, salt, pepper and nutmeg in a saucepan. Beat the egg whites in a bowl until they form stiff peaks.

In a separate saucepan, melt the butter and add the flour. Mix well and cook gently for 1 minute. Next, add the milk mixture slowly, mixing constantly until the texture is smooth and begins to thicken. Add the Parmesan and remaining cheddar. Bring to the boil and simmer for 2 minutes, still stirring constantly. Remove the pan from the heat and allow the mixture to cool slightly before adding the egg yolks. Mix well. Finally, carefully fold in the egg whites.

Remove the ramekins from the fridge and pour in the soufflé mixture. If you wish, extra cheese can be added by half-filling each ramekin, inserting a large cube of cheese, and topping with the remaining mixture.

Place the soufflé dishes in a roasting tin or double boiler and fill with water until it reaches one-third of the way up the dishes. Bake in the oven @ 180°C/gas mark 4 for 30 minutes until well risen and firm. Remove from the oven and allow to cool in the moulds, then store in the fridge overnight.

To reheat, remove the soufflés from the fridge and top with Parmesan. Cook in the oven @ 200°C/gas mark 6 for 12–15 minutes until golden and risen.

110g/4oz mature cheddar – finely grated
275ml/1/2pt milk
2–3 spring onions – finely chopped
pinch salt
pinch freshly ground black pepper
good pinch nutmeg – freshly grated
2 eggs – separated
50g/2oz butter
40g/11/2oz plain flour
50g/2oz Parmesan – grated

4 dsp Parmesan – finely grated

tarragon and paprika cream

Gently heat the cream, paprika, Parmesan and tarragon in a saucepan until the mixture begins to bubble.

Remove the soufflés from the oven and arrange on a plate. Serve immediately surrounded by a little of the tarragon and paprika cream.

275ml/1/2pt double cream
1 tsp paprika
110g/4oz Parmesan
small bunch of fresh tarragon – coarsely chopped

This summery take on the classic meatloaf is perfect for a picnic or light lunch.

summertime
meatloaf

Place all the ingredients except the bacon in a large bowl and mix until everything is well combined.

Line a well-greased loaf tin with half the bacon and place the mixture in the tin. Press down well, then top with the remaining bacon. Cover the loaf tin with tinfoil and place in the oven @ 180°C/gas mark 4 for 1¹/2 hours. Remove the tinfoil and cook uncovered for a further 15 minutes until the bacon is crispy and golden on top. Allow to cool slightly before removing from the tin.

Cut the meat loaf into thick slices and serve warm or cold with a dark leafy salad and a little of the red onion marmalade on page 46.

450g/1lb beef – minced
450g/1lb pork – minced
1 red onion – finely chopped
2 cloves garlic – finely chopped
2 red chillies – deseeded and finely chopped
3–4 eggs – lightly beaten
400g/14oz tin chopped tomatoes – drained
1 dsp basil – chopped
1 dsp parsley – chopped
1 dsp coriander – chopped
50g/2oz Parmesan – grated
8–10 slices streaky bacon

This is a great way to make the flavours of the Mediterranean available all year round.

mediterranean
chutney

Place all the ingredients except the sugar in a large, heavy-based saucepan. Mix well over a gentle heat until the fruit and vegetables begin to soften. Cool slightly, then add the sugar and continue to stir until it has dissolved. Turn up the heat slightly and simmer gently for 1–1½ hours until the chutney begins to thicken and darken in colour. Remove from the heat and set to one side to cool.

Remove the cinnamon sticks and spoon the chutney into sterilised jars, following the instructions for bottling on page 23.

This chutney can be stored for up to 6 months in a cool, dark cupboard.

150ml/¼pt olive oil
450g/1lb tinned chopped tomatoes
1 pear – peeled, cored and diced
1 aubergine – diced
1 courgette – diced
1 medium onion – coarsely
   chopped
110g/4oz sultanas
275ml/½pt cider vinegar
5cm/2 inches fresh ginger – peeled
   and chopped
1 dsp mustard seeds
2 cinnamon sticks – halved
2 chillies – 1 red and one green –
   deseeded and finely chopped
2 tsp salt
225g/8oz soft brown sugar

Add this chutney to casseroles, serve with cooked meats, cheese or salads, or simply spread it on top of warm crusty bread.

tapenade

Place the olive oil, olives, garlic, coriander, capers, salt and pepper in a blender. Whiz slowly until all the ingredients are mixed through. A little more oil can be added for a thinner consistency.

Spoon the tapenade into a bowl and serve.

4 tbsp olive oil
275g/10oz green olives – pitted
good handful coriander
2–3 cloves garlic – finely chopped
50g/2oz capers
pinch sea salt
pinch freshly ground black
   pepper

Tapenade is a rich olive spread that is popular throughout the Mediterranean. There are as many recipes for it as there are uses. Serve with couscous, on top of toast or baked fish or – my own favourite – spread over a rack of lamb before roasting. 55

A lovely idea for a simple snack, fondue is also a great party food.

camembert fondue

serves 4–6

Heat the wine gently in a small saucepan. Add the cheese and allow it to melt slowly, stirring occasionally. Add the garlic and mix gently until all the cheese has completely melted. Do not overheat or the cheese will become stringy.

Pour the fondue into a deep bowl and serve immediately surrounded with vegetable sticks, crackers or tortilla chips.

125ml/4floz French white wine
225g/8oz Camembert – cubed with rind removed
110g/4oz Gruyère or Emmenthal – cubed with rind removed
1 clove garlic – finely chopped

Fondue is traditionally made with two Swiss cheeses, but here I have varied it with creamy French Camembert.

Serve as antipasto or add to sauces for an instant burst of sunshine.

oven-dried cherry tomatoes

makes approximately 900g/2lb

Place the tomatoes cut side down on a baking sheet. Drizzle with a little olive oil and sprinkle with salt. Place in the oven at the lowest setting for 24–48 hours until they have dried out. Times will depend upon the ripeness of the tomatoes.

Put the tomatoes in sterilised jars (see page 23). Pour in the remaining olive oil until the tomatoes are completely covered. Add the fresh basil and seal. The tomatoes can be stored for up to 6 months in a cool, dark cupboard.

900g/2lb cherry tomatoes – halved
1 dsp sea salt
500ml/1pt extra virgin olive oil
good handful basil

Drying tomatoes on a sunny rooftop the traditional Italian way is difficult in our climate. Fortunately, oven-drying them works just as well.

Originally from Tuscany, crostini literally means 'little crusts'.

crostini
with peaches
pears and camembert

serves 2–3

Heat the butter, sugar and honey in a saucepan. Add the peaches and pears and toss around in the hot syrup until well coated and slightly golden, then remove from the heat.

Arrange the bread on a baking tray and place below a hot grill. Toast evenly on both sides. Remove the bread from the grill, drizzle with olive oil, and top with Camembert. Return to the grill until the cheese begins to soften and melt.

Arrange the crostini on individual plates. Using a slotted spoon, top with the peaches and pears. Drizzle with a little of the syrup, sprinkle with pepper and serve immediately.

25g/1oz butter
1 dsp sugar
2 dsp honey
2–3 peaches – stoned and cut into thick slices
2–3 pears – cored and cut into wedges

1 small crusty loaf – thickly sliced
2 dsp olive oil
175g/6oz Camembert – thickly sliced
good pinch freshly ground black pepper

Great for parties and buffets, you can top crostini with lots of different ingredients, such as the country pâté on page 58 or the melon jam on page 23. You should also try varying the type of cheese – Irish Ballyblue makes an unusual and delicious topping.

The colour and texture of this pâté is just glorious. Serve it spread on toast as a light snack or sliced and arranged on a little salad as a starter.

coarse country
pâté

serves 8

Place all the ingredients except the wine in a large bowl and mix well. Add the wine and mix again. Transfer the pâté to a lightly greased loaf tin approximately 13cm/5 inches by 23cm/9 inches. Press down well until the tin is tightly packed. Place the tin in a roasting dish and fill the dish with water until it comes halfway up the tin. Cook in the oven @ 170°C/gas mark 3 for 1 1/2 hours. Remove the pâté from the oven and allow to cool before serving in its own juices.

375g/13oz belly pork – minced
450g/1lb rump steak – minced
250g/9oz lean bacon – finely chopped
1 red chilli – deseeded and finely chopped
4 cloves garlic – finely chopped
pinch salt
pinch freshly ground black pepper
1 tsp peppercorns – coarsely crushed
2 tsp thyme – finely chopped
1 red pepper – deseeded and finely diced
1 green pepper – deseeded and finely diced
110g/4oz mushrooms – finely diced
4 dsp dry white wine

gratin
dauphinois

Remove as much excess starch as possible from the potatoes by placing them in a sieve and rinsing them under a cold tap. Pat the potatoes dry with some kitchen paper.

Butter a shallow, ovenproof dish and arrange the potatoes in layers in the dish. Sprinkle with sea salt.

Gently heat the milk (and cream), garlic and nutmeg in a saucepan until almost boiling. Pour the mixture over the potatoes and sprinkle with cheese. Place the dish in the oven and bake @ 190°C/gas mark 5 for 1–1^3/$_4$ hours until the potatoes are cooked and a golden crust has formed.

Serve hot, garnished with finely chopped chives.

450g/1lb potatoes – peeled and finely sliced
50g/2oz butter
pinch sea salt

275ml/^{1}/$_2$pt milk (or milk and cream)
2 cloves garlic – chopped
^{1}/$_4$ tsp nutmeg – grated
110g/4oz Gruyère – finely grated
1 dsp chives – finely chopped

This makes a delicious meal for vegetarians, served on its own or with a tangy salad. The dish can be made well in advance, or even frozen, as the sauce does not separate.

crispy golden
galettes

Boil the potatoes in a large saucepan for 8–10 minutes until cooked but still firm. Drain, allow to cool slightly, then grate into a large bowl. Add the onion, herbs, nutmeg, seasoning and eggs and mix well.

In a non-stick frying pan, heat the olive oil and butter. Add the potato mixture to the hot pan and press down to form a thin layer. (The mixture can be cooked as one large or several small galettes.) Cook for approximately 3–4 minutes until firm and golden underneath. Flip over and cook the other side for a further 3–4 minutes.

Transfer the galettes to kitchen paper to absorb any excess oil. Arrange the galettes on plates and serve garnished with fresh herbs such as flat-leaf parsley.

3–4 potatoes – peeled and cut in half
^{1}/$_2$ onion – finely chopped
small bunch chives – chopped
small bunch tarragon – chopped
small bunch flat-leaf parsley – chopped
good pinch nutmeg
pinch salt
pinch freshly ground black pepper
2 eggs – lightly beaten
1 tsp olive oil
10g/^{1}/$_2$oz butter

Quick and easy to make, these little potato pancakes make a delicious light lunch, served on their own or topped with a little melting cheese. But I just love them as an accompaniment to any meat dish such as the roasted pork and bean stew on page 87.

Radicchio is an Italian variety of chicory. It is bright red in colour and has an unusual bitter taste that works well with the creamy mozzarella. This dish makes a great vegetarian meal and is an ideal accompaniment to barbecue food.

hot grilled
radicchio
and mozzarella

serves 4

Spread the ciabatta with a little anchovy paste and leave to one side while you prepare the rest of the dish.

Remove any discoloured outer leaves from the radicchio, then cut in half lengthways. Steam gently for 2 minutes, then remove from the heat.

1 ciabatta – thickly sliced
1 dsp anchovy paste or pesto
1–2 heads radicchio – trimmed

Heat the olive oil, butter, balsamic vinegar, chives and seasoning in a large saucepan for 30 seconds. Do not overheat as this will spoil the colour of the chives.

Arrange the radicchio on a grill pan, pour over the sauce and sprinkle with the mozzarella. Flash under a hot grill for approximately 1 minute or until the mozzarella has started to brown.

Arrange the radicchio on top of the ciabatta and sprinkle with Parmesan. Serve immediately.

2 dsp olive oil
25g/1oz butter
2 tbsp balsamic vinegar
2 dsp chives – finely chopped
pinch sea salt
pinch freshly ground black pepper
175g/6oz mozzarella – diced
50g/2oz Parmesan – grated

This chilled Spanish soup is just like a liquid salad. Quick, easy and colourful, it makes a refreshing lunch or light starter for dinner parties.

gazpacho
with garlic croutons

serves 6–8

It is essential to use the freshest and best ingredients available for this soup.

soup

Place all the ingredients except the water in a blender and whiz until very smooth. Transfer the mixture to a large bowl and mix in the water a little at a time. Cover with clingfilm and place in the fridge for at least 1 hour to let the flavours develop.

6 tomatoes – peeled and roughly chopped
2 spring onions – roughly chopped
$1/2$ cucumber – peeled and roughly chopped
2 cloves garlic – crushed
$1/2$ red pepper – deseeded and roughly chopped
pinch salt
pinch freshly ground black pepper
1 tbsp basil – chopped
1 tsp marjoram or oregano – chopped
2 tbsp olive oil
1 tbsp white wine vinegar
275ml/$1/2$pt iced water

garnish

Lightly mix the ingredients for the garnish in a bowl.

$1/2$ green pepper – deseeded and finely diced
$1/4$ cucumber – peeled and diced
2 spring onions – chopped
1 tbsp parsley – coarsely chopped

croutons

Remove the crust and rub the bread with garlic. Cut the bread into cubes approximately 1cm/$1/2$ inch wide and cook in a deep-fat fryer or shallow frying pan for approximately 1–2 minutes until crispy and golden. Transfer the croutons to kitchen paper to remove any excess oil.

Remove the gazpacho from the fridge and pour into soup bowls. Carefully spoon a little garnish into the centre of the soup and sprinkle with croutons.

2 slices white bread
1 clove garlic – halved

This classic French soup has a wonderfully sweet flavour.

onion
soup

serves 5–6

Traditionally topped with Gruyère, you can use any cheese you like – cheddar, goat's cheese and Emmenthal all work well.

soup

Heat the butter and oil in a large saucepan until sizzling. Add the garlic and onions, turn down the heat and cook slowly for 5–6 minutes until the onions have softened and started to caramelise. Next, add the salt, pepper, paprika, stock and wine and cook over a low heat for a further 45 minutes.

25g/1oz butter
1 dsp olive oil
3 cloves garlic – chopped
700g/1 1/2lb onions – sliced
pinch salt
pinch freshly ground black pepper
1/2 tsp paprika
750ml/1 1/3pt beef stock
275ml/1/2pt white wine

topping

Ladle the soup into bowls. Butter the bread and carefully arrange a few slices on top of the soup, then sprinkle with cheese. Place the bowls beneath a hot grill or use a blowtorch and heat until the cheese is bubbling and golden. Serve immediately.

1 baguette – sliced
25g/1oz butter
110g/4oz Gruyère – grated

This wholesome Italian soup is packed full of fresh vegetables. For a vegetarian version, simply leave out the bacon and use vegetable stock.

minestrone

Heat the butter and oil in a saucepan until hot and sizzling. Add the garlic and bacon and cook for 3–4 minutes until the bacon is crispy. Next, add the onion, celery and carrots and cook for a further 3–4 minutes. Finally, add the tomatoes and the sundried tomato paste and mix well. Place a lid on the saucepan and reduce the temperature. Leave to simmer for 10 minutes.

25g/1oz butter
1 tbsp olive oil
2–3 cloves garlic – crushed
2 rashers streaky bacon – chopped
1 onion – finely chopped
3 stalks celery – finely chopped
2 carrots – finely chopped
400g/14oz tin chopped tomatoes
1 dsp sundried tomato paste

Now add the stock, leeks, pasta, salt, pepper and half the herbs. Replace the lid and cook for a further 10–12 minutes.

1 litre/1³/4pt chicken or vegetable stock
1 leek – finely chopped
110g/4oz pasta
pinch salt
pinch freshly ground black pepper
2 tbsp basil – finely chopped
2 tbsp flat-leaf parsley – finely chopped

Just before serving, add the remainder of the herbs and stir well. Spoon into bowls and serve immediately sprinkled with a little Parmesan.

110g/4oz Parmesan – shaved

Any type of pasta can be used in this soup, but I find that fine tubular pastas work best.

fish

A **great source** of **nutrients**, fish is a **delicious** and healthy fast food. Grill, bake, stew or even barbecue for an authentic Mediteranean experience. A real treat all year round.

oven-baked **mussels** with pistou

Mussels have a natural sweetness and go well with many different flavours. I love the texture of them baked in this way and garnished with pistou. The main work involved in this dish is in the preparation of the mussels. Always buy fresh mussels and discard any broken or open shells. Remove the beard and give them a good scrub before cooking.

Place the cleaned, prepared mussels in a large, shallow saucepan and add the wine, stock, garlic, saffron and salt. Cover and simmer over a medium heat for 5–6 minutes – do not boil rapidly. Drain the mussels and reserve the juices. Discard any mussels that have not opened and arrange the remainder in a single layer on a large ovenproof platter. The mussels are ready to eat at this stage and can be served with just the pistou if desired.

1.5kg/3^1/2lb mussels
275ml/^{1}/2pt dry white wine
275ml/^{1}/2pt fish stock
2–3 cloves garlic – coarsely chopped
^{1}/2 tsp saffron powder
^{1}/2 tsp sea salt

Heat 1 dsp of olive oil in a pan, add the onion and cook for 2–3 minutes. Add the bacon or ham along with the lemon, capers and parsley and cook for a further 2–3 minutes. Finally, add the breadcrumbs and cook until the crumbs are well coated. Top each mussel with a spoonful of this mixture, sprinkle with the remaining olive oil and bake in the oven @ 200°C/gas mark 6 for 10–12 minutes.

2 dsp olive oil
1 small onion – finely chopped
50g/2oz bacon or Parma ham – finely chopped
zest and juice of 1 lemon
50g/2oz capers
1 dsp parsley – coarsely chopped
110g/4oz white breadcrumbs

Boil the reserved juices in the saucepan until reduced by two-thirds. Remove the mussels from the oven and drizzle with the jus. Serve immediately with generous dollops of pistou and crusty French bread.

pistou

Pistou is basically a French version of pesto, though pistou is traditionally coarser in texture.

Place all the ingredients in a blender and whiz to form a coarse paste. The pistou can be made smoother by continuing to whiz a little longer, but it may need a little extra olive oil.

4 cloves garlic – coarsely chopped
2 handfuls basil leaves – shredded
125ml/4floz olive oil
50g/2oz Parmesan or Gruyère – grated
pinch freshly ground black pepper
pinch sea salt

Crunchy on the outside, moist on the inside, this light fish dish also works well with fillets of plaice, halibut or whiting.

crusted
lemon sole
in a white wine sauce

serves 4

lemon sole

Skin the lemon sole fillets and cut into thick strips. Place on a plate and scatter with the parsley and Parmesan. Pat down well, then turn the fish over and repeat.

Add the olive oil and butter to a shallow frying pan and heat over a low temperature. Arrange the fish in the pan flesh side down and cook gently for 2–3 minutes on each side, turning only once until the fish is a light golden brown. Remove the fish from the pan and place on kitchen paper to absorb any excess oil.

4–6 lemon sole fillets
4 dsp parsley – finely chopped
110g/4oz Parmesan – finely grated
1 dsp olive oil
25g/1oz butter
zest and juice of 2 lemons

white wine sauce

Pour the cream and milk into a cold bowl and beat together until frothy but not thick. This should take approximately 4–5 minutes. Melt the butter in a saucepan and add the milk and cream along with the wine. Heat very gently and add the salt, pepper and paprika to taste. When the sauce begins to thicken slightly, remove the pan from the heat and set to one side.

125ml/4floz whipping cream
2 dsp milk
125ml/4floz dry white wine
25g/1oz butter
good pinch sea salt
good pinch freshly ground black pepper
good pinch paprika

Arrange the fish on an ovenproof serving dish, top with the white wine sauce and sprinkle with Parmesan. Flash under a hot grill until bubbling and brown. Serve garnished with wedges of lemon and accompanied by seasonal vegetables such as asparagus or petits pois.

25g/1oz Parmesan – finely grated
1 lemon – cut into wedges

You can use lots of different combinations of fish in this recipe depending upon availability. The underlying flavour of the Mediterranean is provided by the broth – a fragrant mixture of garlic, chillies, tomato paste, saffron and herbs.

fish
stew

serves 6

fish

Prepare the fish according to your selection. Clams can be cooked in their shells, but discard any that are slightly open before cooking or remain closed after cooking. Wash all the fish well before using.

700g/1 1/2lb assorted fish, e.g. mullet, monkfish, halibut, bass, marlin, swordfish
700g/1 1/2lb assorted shellfish, e.g. langoustines, scallops, clams
mixed herbs to garnish, e.g. parsley and basil

broth

Prepare the saffron by placing the threads in the warm water for 10–12 minutes to infuse.

Heat the oil in a large heavy-based saucepan and add the garlic and chillies. Cook for 2–3 minutes. Add the onions, celery and tomatoes and cook for a further 8–10 minutes, stirring occasionally. Next, add the salt, pepper, fish stock, wine, tomato paste, pesto and potatoes. Strain the liquid from the saffron and add it to the pan. Stir well. Cover and leave to simmer gently for 12–15 minutes.

Carefullly lower the fish into the pot. Cover, reduce the heat and cook for another 7–8 minutes.

Adjust the seasoning to taste and garnish with the herbs. This stew is delicious topped with a dollop of the rouille on page 74 and accompanied by the flat olive oil soda bread on page 17.

10–12 threads saffron
3–4 tbsp warm water

2 dsp olive oil
2 cloves garlic – finely chopped
2–3 red chillies – deseeded and chopped
2 onions – cut into chunks
2 stalks celery – cut into chunks
6 tomatoes – skinned, deseeded and chopped
pinch salt
pinch freshly ground black pepper
275ml/1/2pt fish stock
275ml/1/2pt white wine
4 tsp tomato paste
1 tsp red pesto
10–12 baby potatoes – cut in half
mixed herbs to garnish

A good fish pie depends on the mix of the ingredients and the freshness and quality of the potatoes.

fish
with garlic and
parmesan potatoes

serves 4

Peel the potatoes and cut them into 1cm/^{1}/2 inch-thick slices. Steam for 10 minutes.

6 potatoes

Cut the fish into bite-sized pieces and place in a lightly greased ovenproof dish. Scatter the prawns over the fish and sprinkle with the spring onions and lemon zest and juice. Dot with butter and pour over the cream.

225g/8oz white fish – skinned
225g/8oz undyed smoked fish – skinned
110g/4oz cooked prawns – peeled
2 dsp spring onions – peeled
zest and juice of 1 lemon
25g/1oz butter
275ml/^{1}/2pt whipping cream

Place the potatoes, garlic and Parmesan in a bowl and mix well. Spread the potatoes over the top of the fish and season. Bake in the oven @ 200°C/gas mark 6 for 20–25 minutes.

2 cloves garlic – finely chopped
110g/4oz Parmesan shavings
pinch salt
pinch freshly ground black pepper

Serve hot, garnished with chives or parsley.

1–2 dsp chives or parsley – finely chopped

Rouille is a spicy garlic mayonnaise from the south of France. A traditional accompaniment to fish soups and stews, I like to spread it generously over crisp, salty sardines for a mouthwatering combination of textures and flavours.

grilled sardines
on wheaten bread
with rouille

serves 4–6

rouille

Place all the ingredients except the olive oil in a blender. Whiz well until the mixture is very smooth and creamy. Very slowly drizzle in the oil, whizzing all the time, until the mixture resembles a mayonnaise. Pour the rouille into a serving bowl and place in the fridge to set for at least 30 minutes.

3–4 cloves garlic – finely chopped
1 egg yolk
2 dsp groundnut oil
1/2 tsp paprika
1/2 tsp saffron powder
pinch salt
pinch freshly ground black pepper
juice of 1 lemon or lime
125ml/4floz olive oil

grilled sardines

Prepare the fish. You can ask your fishmonger to do this for you; otherwise it is fairly easy when the fish are large and fresh. Using a sharp knife, scrape the scales from the sardines, then slit along the underside of each fish and remove the intestines. Cut off the heads and place the fish on a chopping board skin side up. Press along the backbone with your thumb, then turn the fish over and lift away the backbone. Rinse the sardines well under a cold tap and dry well with kitchen paper. Coat the sardines with sea salt and pat down. Leave the fish to sit for 1–2 minutes, then shake or brush off any excess salt.

12 fresh plump sardines
1–2 dsp sea salt
1 dsp olive oil

Heat a lightly oiled grill pan and cook the sardines under a medium grill for approximately 6–8 minutes depending upon size, turning occasionally.

Arrange the sardines on thick slices of wheaten bread and top with rouille. Serve immediately with wedges of lemon.

4–6 slices wheaten bread
1 lemon – cut into wedges

I love this combination of light, fragrant risotto and hot spicy prawns. Use a good quality, low salt stock for best results.

tangy lime risotto with hot spicy prawns

serves 4–6

risotto

Heat together the olive oil and half the butter in a large saucepan. Add the onion, salt and lime zest and stir continuously for approximately 4–5 minutes until the onions are translucent. Next, add the rice and stir for 2–3 minutes until well coated. Add the stock a little at a time, stirring well with each addition, until it has been absorbed. Finally, add the lime juice, pepper and the remainder of the butter and stir through. Turn off the heat, cover and leave to infuse for 3–4 minutes.

1 tbsp olive oil
50g/2oz butter
1 onion – finely chopped
pinch salt
zest of 1 lime
275g/10oz arborio rice
850ml/1 1/2pt chicken stock
1 tbsp lime juice
good pinch freshly ground black pepper

hot spicy prawns

Grind the chillies, garlic and olive oil in a pestle and mortar until you have an almost smooth paste. Transfer the mixture to a saucepan and heat for 2–3 minutes, then add the salt, pepper and prawns. Turn up the heat until the oil is sizzling and cook until the prawns have warmed through.

2 red chillies – deseeded and finely chopped
1 green chilli – deseeded and finely chopped
2 cloves garlic – finely chopped
2 dsp olive oil
pinch sea salt
pinch freshly ground black pepper
450g/1lb cooked large prawns – shelled

Spoon the risotto into shallow bowls, top with prawns and garnish with coriander and lime. Serve immediately.

small bunch coriander – finely chopped
1 lime – cut into wedges

Sardines always remind me of summer holidays in the south of France, where they are cooked and eaten fresh from the boats. Quick and easy to make, I think this recipe captures some of that Mediterranean spirit.

barbecued
sardines
with herbs
and lime mayo

serves 4–6

lime mayonnaise

Place the eggs, mustard, garlic, salt and pepper in a food processor and whiz very slowly. Slowly drizzle in the oil while continuing to whiz. Finally, add the vinegar. When the mixture is well combined, taste and, if you wish, add a little more vinegar to sharpen the flavour. Transfer the mixture to a jar, cover tightly and chill in the fridge for at least 2 hours before serving.

2 eggs
1/2 tsp English mustard
1 clove garlic – crushed
pinch freshly ground black pepper
125ml lightly flavoured oil, e.g.
  grapeseed
1 dsp white wine vinegar

Mix together the mayonnaise, lime and sea salt in a small bowl, then add a sprinkling of paprika. Place in the fridge to chill while you prepare and cook the sardines.

zest and juice of 1 lime
1 tsp sea salt
pinch paprika

sardines

Prepare the fish according to the instructions on page 74, or ask your fishmonger to do it for you. Next, sprinkle the sardines with salt, pepper and the lemon zest and juice and pat down well. Place the sardines on a barbecue or arrange on a lightly oiled grill pan and place under a hot grill. Cook for 2 minutes on each side, turning only once to prevent the sardines breaking up.

2 tbsp olive oil
900g/2lb fresh sardines
1–2 tsp sea salt
pinch freshly ground black
  pepper
zest and juice of 1 lemon

Remove the sardines from the heat and serve immediately with lime mayonnaise, baked potatoes and a little green salad.

meat

From **hearty, slow-cooked** casseroles and stews to tasty chops and steaks ready in minutes, Mediterranean cuisine is all about **minimum fuss** and **maximum pleasure**. Enjoy with good company and a glass of wine.

Duck is great with citrus flavours; in this recipe I have also added sweet Marsala wine and redcurrant jelly to create a vivid, ruby-red jus.

pan-fried
duck
with baby onions
orange and marsala

serves 4

The breast is the leanest part of the duck and can be cooked in many ways – grilled, poached or sautéed.

Score the skin of the duck in a criss-cross fashion so it can release its juices. Melt the butter in a frying pan and cook the duck breasts skin side down over a medium heat for 6–8 minutes until the skin is crisp and golden. Drain any fat from the pan and turn the duck breasts over. Turn down the temperature and continue to cook the duck over a low heat for 4–5 minutes.

4 duck breasts – skin on
25g/1oz butter

When the duck has almost finished its initial cooking, boil the baby onions in a small saucepan for 10–12 minutes until slightly softened. Drain and add the onions to the duck along with the cloves of garlic.

225g/8oz baby onions – peeled
2 cloves garlic – peeled

Using a sharp knife, peel the oranges and carefully remove the pith and pips. Cut into segments, retaining any juice.

2 oranges
good bunch fresh thyme
125ml/4floz Marsala wine
1 dsp redcurrant jelly
pinch salt
pinch freshly ground black
   pepper

Pour the Marsala wine over the duck breasts and add the thyme, redcurrant jelly and any orange juice left over from the segmenting. This will thicken the sauce slightly and create the glaze. Let the mixture bubble gently for a few minutes, then add the orange segments. Taste and season as required and remove from the heat.

Slice the duck breasts and arrange on individual plates. Using a slotted spoon, add some of the oranges and the onions and drizzle with the Marsala and redcurrant jus. Finally, garnish with sprigs of thyme.
Serve immediately with the crispy potato galettes on page 60 to mop up the juices.

sprigs of thyme to garnish

This is one of those brilliantly simple dishes where the marinade also works as a sauce. The fresh lemony flavours go really well with baked potatoes, asparagus and, of course, lots of bread to mop up the sauce.

sticky
lemon chicken
with asparagus

serves 4

lemon chicken

Score the skin of the chicken, dust with flour, salt and pepper and pat down well. In a large shallow saucepan, heat the oil and butter until hot and sizzling. Add the chicken pieces, skin side first if using breasts, and cook, turning occasionally until the chicken is golden and crispy. Turn the heat down, cover and leave to cook for approximately 20–25 minutes depending upon the size of the chicken pieces. When cooked through, lift the chicken out of the pan and set to one side.

4 chicken portions – wings, legs, breasts or thighs (skin on)
25g/1oz plain flour
pinch salt
pinch freshly ground black pepper
4 dsp olive oil
25g/1oz butter

Turn the heat up and add the lemon juice and garlic to the pan along with a little extra butter if required. Stir continuously. Next, add the honey and wine and return the chicken pieces to the pan. Simmer gently for 5–6 minutes.

juice of 2 large lemons
2 cloves garlic – crushed
125ml/4floz honey
1 glass white wine

asparagus

Snap off and discard the woody ends of the asparagus, leaving the tender tips. Bring a pan of salted water to the boil and carefully place the asparagus into it. Cook uncovered for approximately 6 minutes, adjusting the cooking time depending on the thickness of the spears, but be careful not to overcook or the colour will spoil. The best way to test asparagus is to place a skewer through the thickest part of the stalk – if the skewer passes through easily, the asparagus is ready. Drain and add to the chicken and lemon sauce.

225g/8oz green asparagus

Serve immediately garnished with parsley.

2–3 tbsp flat-leaf parsley – chopped

Passata, a sieved tomato pureé with a very intense flavour, is the basis of this simple casserole from the Basque region of Spain. It can be made with chicken breasts or legs, but I like it best made from a whole chicken, jointed and with the skin left on.

poulet
basquaise

serves 6

Heat 2 dsp olive oil in a large saucepan. Add the chicken, skin side down, and cook for approximately 10–12 minutes, turning occasionally, until the chicken is crispy and golden brown. Remove the chicken from the pan and set to one side.

Heat the remainder of the olive oil in the saucepan. Add the onion, garlic, peppers, chillies and bay leaf and cook for 5–6 minutes, then add the tomato paste, tomatoes, passata and wine. Simmer the sauce for a further 8–10 minutes.

Return the chicken and any juices to the saucepan. Top up with stock until the chicken is completely covered with liquid and mix well. Sprinkle the casserole with parsley and season with salt and pepper. Turn the temperature down as low as possible, cover and simmer very slowly for 1 hour and 20 minutes. Alternatively, the casserole can be placed in the oven at 220°C/gas mark 7 for 1–1 1/2 hours. Add the olives and cook for a further 10 minutes.

Remove the casserole from the heat and take out the bay leaf. Serve immediately on a bed of pasta, rice or the baked couscous on page 35.

4 dsp olive oil
1 jointed chicken – 1.8kg/4lb

6 small onions – peeled and cut in half
2 cloves garlic – finely chopped
4 peppers – 2 red and 2 yellow – deseeded and cut into large chunks
2 chillies – 1 red and 1 green – deseeded and finely chopped
1 bay leaf
125ml/4floz sundried tomato paste
4 large tomatoes – quartered
125ml/4floz passata
250ml/8floz dry white wine
570ml/1pt chicken stock
2 tbsp parsley – chopped
pinch salt
pinch freshly ground black pepper
150g/5oz assorted olives – pitted

This sauce works well with both lamb and pork chops. Apricots have a very short season, but peaches and nectarines make good substitutes. Serve with a green salad and the flat olive oil soda bread on page 17.

grilled chops
with apricot and orange sauce

serves 4

apricot and orange sauce

Place all the ingredients in a saucepan and mix well. Bring to the boil, then reduce the heat and simmer gently for 12–15 minutes. If liked, the sauce can then be quickly whizzed in a blender to give it a smoother consistency.

375g/13oz apricots
2 tbsp sundried tomato paste
zest and juice of 1 orange
2 dsp soy sauce
2 dsp Worcestershire sauce
2–3 cloves garlic – finely chopped
25g/1oz soft brown sugar
5cm/2 inches ginger – peeled and grated
1/4 onion – finely chopped

grilled chops

Add the butter and oil to a large frying pan and heat until very hot. Add the chops and cook for 1–2 minutes on both sides until golden. Reduce the heat and cook gently, turning occasionally, until the meat is tender. Cooking times will depend on the thickness of the chops, but pork chops will take approximately 15–20 minutes, and lamb chops will take 10–15 minutes.

Remove the chops from the pan and brush with the apricot and orange sauce. Flash the chops under a very hot grill or place on the barbecue until the sauce is bubbling and slightly blackened. Serve immediately with the remainder of the sauce on the side.

10g/1/2oz butter
1 dsp olive oil
4 loin chops – lamb or pork

Rustic and wholesome, this light stew is perfect for casual eating. When the stew is cooked through, I like to crumble a little feta cheese over the dish and pop it under the grill.

summer stew
of chorizo, green peppers,
potato and herbs

Heat the olive oil in a large saucepan. Add the garlic cloves and chorizo and cook together until the chorizo has softened slightly. Next, add the potatoes, peppers, onion, tomato paste and soy sauce and mix well. Continue to cook the mixture for 8–10 minutes, stirring occasionally, until the vegetables are well coloured. Add the cayenne pepper, bay leaf, mustard, stock and half the parsley and stir again. Cover, turn down the heat and leave to simmer for 25–30 minutes or until the potatoes have cooked through.

Remove the stew from the hob and take out the bay leaf. Garnish with the remainder of the parsley and serve immediately with nutmeg and mustard mash.

125ml/4floz olive oil
2 cloves garlic – peeled
225g/8oz chorizo – thickly sliced
900g/2lb potatoes – cut into large chunks
2 green peppers – deseeded and cut into large chunks
2 onions – cut into small chunks
1 dsp sundried tomato paste
1 dsp soy sauce
1/2 tsp cayenne pepper
1 bay leaf
1 tsp Dijon mustard
125ml/4floz vegetable stock
good bunch flat-leaf parsley – coarsely chopped

nutmeg and
mustard mash

Cook the potatoes in a saucepan of boiling salted water for 15–20 minutes or until tender. Drain and mash well, then cover to keep the mash warm.

In a separate pan, heat together the milk, butter, pepper, nutmeg and mustard. Allow the mixture to warm through, then add to the potatoes. Mix well and adjust the seasoning to taste. Serve hot, garnished with flat-leaf parsley.

6–8 floury potatoes – peeled and cut into chunks
pinch salt
150ml/1/4pt milk
50g/2oz butter
pinch freshly ground black pepper
1/4 tsp nutmeg – grated
1/2 tsp French mustard
small handful flat-leaf parsley – coarsely chopped

There are many different versions of this dish and different combinations of vegetables can be used according to the season. Although not quite authentic, tinned haricot beans can be used instead of dried – as they are pre-cooked, the preparation time will be greatly reduced.

roasted
pork and bean
stew

serves 4–6

Soak the dried haricot beans in cold water overnight, then drain, place in a large saucepan, cover with water and bring to the boil. Simmer for 1 hour, then drain again and set to one side to cool.

700g/1 1/2lb dried white haricot beans

Trim any excess fat off the pork shoulder, roll and tie securely with string. Crisp the belly pork or bacon in a large, heavy-based saucepan – there is no need to add oil. Add the pork shoulder and roll around the pan to brown the sides and seal in the flavour. Add the whole garlic cloves, star anise, thyme, peppercorns, onions, leeks, carrots and whole turnips. Toss around to coat all the ingredients, allowing them to turn slightly golden. This should take approximately 10 minutes.

1.8kg/4lb shoulder of pork
450g/1lb belly pork or streaky bacon – chopped
25g/1oz butter
1 dsp olive oil
4 cloves garlic – peeled
1 star anise
bunch of fresh thyme
small handful mixed peppercorns
2 large onions – quartered
4 leeks – sliced
4 carrots – cut into large chunks
4 small white/pink turnips
570ml/1pt stock
1 bay leaf

Add the stock, beans and bay leaf, cover and simmer for 2–2 1/2 hours.

Mix the mustards and herbs. Take the pork out of the pan and remove the string. Spread the mustard mixture over the pork. Return the pork to the pan and simmer for a further 10 minutes.

1 tsp English mustard
1 tsp French mustard
1 tsp wholegrain mustard
1 tbsp parsley – coarsely chopped
1 tbsp fresh chives – coarsely chopped

Remove the pork from the pan and serve on a platter with the stewed vegetables and the crispy golden galettes on page 60 arranged around the outside.

The secret of really tasty lamb shanks is in the cooking – brown quickly to seal in the flavour, then roast slowly in the oven. The lamb will become so tender it will almost fall off the bone.

mediterranean
lamb
shanks

Trim off any excess fat from the lamb shanks. Dust well with flour on all sides and pat down. Heat half the the olive oil in a large ovenproof pot. Add the lamb and brown well on all sides, turning occasionally. Remove the lamb from the dish and set to one side.

4 small lamb shanks
25g/1oz plain flour
75ml/3floz olive oil

Place the vegetables in a large bowl and add the remaining olive oil. Mix until the vegetables are well coated, then add to the pot and cook until golden. This should take approximately 15–20 minutes. If the aubergine soaks up a lot of the oil, more may be added.

2 cloves garlic – coarsely chopped
2 large onions – cut into chunks
1 aubergine – cut into chunks
2 yellow peppers – deseeded and cut into chunks
2 courgettes – cut into chunks
400g/14oz tin chopped tomatoes
2 tsp harissa paste
1 dsp tomato purée
125ml/4floz vegetable stock

Add the tomatoes, harissa and tomato purée and cook for a further 2–3 minutes until the vegetables start to reduce down to a soft stew. Return the lamb shanks to the pot and mix well. Add enough stock to completely immerse the shanks and stir again. Cover and cook in the oven @ 170°C/gas mark 3 for 2–2 1/2 hours.

Remove the casserole from the oven. Add a few black olives if liked and adjust the seasoning according to taste. Garnish generously with parsley and serve immediately with bread, pasta, or the nutmeg and mustard mash on page 86.

50g/2oz black olives – pitted (optional)
good pinch freshly ground black pepper
pinch salt
4 dsp flat-leaf parsley – coarsely chopped

Harissa is a fiery chilli sauce from Tunisia – use with care! It is available from most large supermarkets and delicatessens as a sauce, powder or paste.

Part of the success of this dish lies with the choice of a good red wine. I would recommend a dry wine such such as Cabernet Sauvignon.

beef casserole
in red wine
with pine nuts and sultanas

serves 6–8

If you would prefer not to use wine, then good-quality beef stock also works very well.

This dish can either be cooked in the oven or on the hob. Heat the oil in a heavy-based pan and add the onion, carrot, celery and bay leaves and cook for 8–10 minutes, stirring occasionally to prevent the vegetables sticking.

In a separate pan, melt the butter until hot and sizzling and add the steak pieces. Add the chillies and garlic and continue to cook for 8–10 minutes. When the meat has browned, add the red wine, thyme, pine nuts and sultanas. Mix well, then add the lightly cooked vegetables. Simmer gently on the hob or cook in the oven @ 200°C/gas mark 6 for 1 3/4–2 hours. Stir occasionally. You may need to add a little extra stock or red wine during cooking. Serve hot, with warm crusty bread, and garnished with flat-leaf parsley.

2 dsp olive oil
1 red onion – coarsely sliced
1 onion – coarsely sliced
1 carrot – finely chopped
4 stalks celery – finely chopped
2 bay leaves
25g/1oz butter
450g/1lb steak pieces – cut into
    2.5cm/1 inch cubes
1 red and 1 green chilli – deseeded
    and finely chopped
2 cloves garlic – finely chopped
275ml/1/2pt red wine
1 dsp thyme – chopped
75g/3oz pine nuts
75g/3oz sultanas
small bunch flat-leaf parsley –
    roughly chopped

A classic wine-based stew from the Provence region of France. Traditionally accompanied by macaroni or noodles, I like to serve it with the gratin dauphinois on page 60.

boeuf
en daube

serves 6

Mix the wine, bay leaves, peppercorns, salt and mustard in a large bowl. Add the steak pieces and cover with clingfilm. Marinate for 4–6 hours, or overnight if possible, then remove the beef with a slotted spoon, retaining the marinade.

425ml/^{3}/$_4$pt full-bodied red wine
4 bay leaves
small handful mixed peppercorns – lightly crushed
pinch sea salt
1–2 tsp Dijon mustard
900g–1.3kg/2–3lb rump steak – cubed

In a large saucepan, heat three-quarters of the olive oil and add the garlic and onions. Sauté well for 4–5 minutes. Add the marinade and half the flour and stir well over a low heat to avoid lumps. Finally, stir in the orange zest and tomatoes, cover and leave to simmer for 6–7 minutes.

125ml/4floz olive oil
2–3 cloves garlic – finely chopped
2 onions – sliced
50g/2oz flour
zest of 1 orange
625g/1lb 6oz tinned chopped tomatoes

Heat the rest of the olive oil in a frying pan. Dust the marinated steak pieces in the remaining flour and add to the pan. Cook over a medium heat to brown and seal in the flavour. This will take approximately 8–10 minutes.

Take the frying pan off the heat and add the beef and any juices to the saucepan containing the sauce. Mix well. Add a little beef stock to adjust the consistency as required. Cover and place in the oven for 1 hour at 170°C/gas mark 3.

beef stock – as required

Remove the casserole from the oven and add the carrots, mushrooms and olives. Cover and return to the oven for another hour.

4–6 carrots – sliced
225g/8oz mushrooms – quartered
black olives – optional

Adjust the seasoning to taste and garnish with parsley. Serve immediately with the crispy potato galettes on page 60 to mop up the juices.

pinch salt
pinch freshly ground black pepper
small handful flat-leaf parsley – chopped

There is simply nothing nicer than a perfectly cooked steak. This combination of steak and the creamy, salty tang of Roquefort works a treat.

steak
with creamy roquefort and tarragon sauce

serves 2

steak

Lightly sprinkle a grill pan with olive oil and pepper and heat to a high temperature. Spread the mustard lightly over the steaks and add the steaks to the pan. Cook for the desired length of time, turning once.

1 dsp olive oil
pinch freshly ground black pepper
1 tsp Dijon mustard
2 fillet steaks – approximately 150g/5oz each

roquefort and tarragon sauce

Heat the olive oil and butter in a shallow saucepan. Add the spring onions and cook for 1 minute. Now add the wine and boil rapidly for 1 minute – the mixture should start to reduce. Turn down the heat and add the cream, pepper and cheese, stirring occasionally. Allow the sauce to heat through gently until the cheese shows signs of melting. Add the tarragon and stir well. Finally, taste the sauce and add a little salt if required.

1 dsp olive oil
25g/1oz butter
2 spring onions – finely chopped
125ml/4floz white wine
125 ml/4floz double cream
pinch freshly ground black pepper
110g/4oz Roquefort – crumbled
small bunch tarragon – coarsely shredded
pinch salt

In a separate frying pan, lightly toss the mushrooms and asparagus spears in a little melted butter for approximately 1 minute.

110g/4oz assorted mushrooms
110g/4oz green asparagus
10g/½oz butter

Serve the steaks topped with the lightly sautéed vegetables and pour over the sauce. The gratin dauphinois on page 60 goes very well with this.

Cook the steak for 1 minute on each side for a rare steak; 3 minutes each side for medium; and 4–5 minutes on each side for well-done.

Made entirely from ewe's milk, this famous blue cheese is aired and ripened in caves under the village of Roquefort-sur-Soulzon in southern France.

Béarnaise sauce has a reputation for being hard to make, but the trick is to whisk the sauce constantly to prevent it from separating. It is also great with asparagus, artichokes and fish.

peppered
steak
with béarnaise sauce

serves 2

steak

Lightly sprinkle a grill pan with the olive oil and peppercorns and heat to a high temperature. Cook the steak for 1 minute on each side for a rare steak; 3 minutes each side for medium; and 4–5 minutes on each side for well-done. Cuts like rib eye may take slighty longer to cook than fillet steaks.

1 dsp black peppercorns – crushed
1 dsp olive oil
2 rib eye steaks – approximately 150g/5oz each

béarnaise sauce

Slowly melt the butter in a small saucepan, skimming off any residue that rises to the surface. Remove from the heat and allow to settle, then pour off the top layer of clear liquid, retaining only the milky liquid.

In a separate saucepan, mix the vinegar, wine, shallot, bay leaf, peppercorns and half the tarragon. Bring to the boil and simmer for 2–3 minutes until the mixture has reduced by one third.

200g/7oz unsalted butter
1 tbsp white wine vinegar
1–2 tbsp dry white wine
1 shallot – finely chopped
1 bay leaf
6–8 white peppercorns – crushed
small sprig tarragon

Strain the liquid into a bowl and place the bowl over a saucepan of warm, not hot, water. Add the eggs and whisk over a medium heat for 5–6 minutes until the mixture is smooth and creamy. Reduce the heat and gradually add the butter, whisking continuously. Finally, add the lemon juice and the remainder of the tarragon and mix well.

4 egg yolks
juice of 1/2 lemon

Remove the steaks from the pan, arrange on plates and allow to rest for 1 minute. Pour over a little of the béarnaise sauce and serve with seasonal vegetables and the gratin dauphinois on page 60.

This classic French dish is made with chicken, onions, mushrooms and red wine. You can use any combination of chicken wings, thighs, breasts or legs, but leave the skin on for extra flavour – and a few more calories!

coq
au vin

Heat the butter and oil in a large frying pan until hot and sizzling. Add the chicken joints skin side down, and cook for 3–4 minutes until crispy and brown. Turn the chicken over and cook for a further 3–4 minutes. Remove from the pan and place in a large saucepan.

25g/1oz butter
1 tbsp olive oil
6–8 chicken joints – skin on

Add the onions, bacon, thyme, garlic and mushrooms to the frying pan and cook for 3–4 minutes – there is no need to add extra oil. Next, add the bay leaves and wine and cook for a further 5–6 minutes. Transfer the entire mixture to the large saucepan, cover and cook over a gentle heat for 1 hour.

350g/12oz baby onions
110g/4oz bacon – diced
1 tsp thyme
2 cloves garlic – chopped
350g/12oz mushrooms – coarsely chopped
2 bay leaves
275ml/^{1}/2pt red wine

When the hour is up, mix the flour and butter in a small bowl. Stir the mixture into the casserole and cook for a further 10–15 minutes. Remove the bay leaves and garnish with parsley. Serve immediately with warm crusty bread or mashed potatoes.

1 tbsp plain flour
25g/1oz butter – softened
small bunch parsley – finely chopped

desserts

From **light and tangy** mango sorbet to **wickedly indulgent** dark choclate tart, the people of the Mediterranean have a sensible attitude to **the sweeter things in life**. So go on – **treat yourself.**

Panna cotta is a traditional Italian pudding meaning 'cooked cream'. It can be subtly flavoured with a range of ingredients – try coffee, chocolate, caramel or vanilla. Here I have opted for fresh fruit flavours.

lemon and rosehip

panna cotta

with

spiced crab apples

serves 4

Rosehips are the berry-like fruit of the rose plant. Naturally high in vitamins A and C, they are believed to delay the effects of ageing. Rosehip syrup is available in large supermarkets and health food stores, or you can make your own. Simply top and tail 225g/8oz of rosehips and add them to 570ml/1pt of water along with 110g/4oz of caster sugar. Simmer rapidly for 30 minutes, strain and leave to cool.

panna cotta

Gently heat the milk, cream and sugar in a small saucepan until the sugar has fully dissolved. Add the vanilla, lemon juice and rosehip syrup and remove from the heat. Set to one side for 15–20 minutes to let the flavours infuse.

Return the saucepan to the heat and simmer gently for 5 minutes but do not allow to boil. Leave to one side to cool slightly. If using powdered gelatine, place the powder in a small bowl and add 2 dsp of cold water. Place the bowl over a small saucepan of hot water until the gelatine dissolves into a clear syrupy liquid. Add the gelatine to the cream mixture and stir well. Pour the mixture into lightly greased individual moulds approximately 5cm/2 inches in diameter. Allow to cool, then cover with clingfilm and chill in the refrigerator for 2–3 hours until set.

150ml/¼pt full-cream milk
275ml/½pt double cream
110g/4oz caster sugar
few drops vanilla essence
juice of 1 lemon
dash rosehip syrup
25g/1oz gelatine
2 dsp cold water

spiced crab apples

Place all the ingredients in a large saucepan and bring to the boil. Simmer for 2–3 minutes, then leave to one side to cool slightly.

Remove the moulds from the fridge and place in a basin of warm water for 30 seconds. Then turn them gently upside down onto your serving plate and the moulds should come away easily. Using a slotted spoon, arrange some of the crab apples around the panna cotta and pour over a little syrup.
Serve immediately.

200g/7oz crab apples or
 small eating apples –
 cored and halved
50ml/2floz cold water
½ tsp cinnamon powder
small handful cloves
110g/4oz demerara sugar

This is a lovely way to cook and serve pears as it really brings out the sweet, spicy flavour of the fruit. The colour is fantastic too.

pears
poached
in honey and red wine

Place the wine, honey, cloves, cinnamon stick, mace and sugar in a small saucepan and stir well. Bring to the boil, then reduce the heat and leave to simmer for ten minutes.

Cut a fine slice from the base of the pears so they will sit steadily during cooking and place them in an ovenproof dish – you need a dish in which the pears can be poached upright and almost completely covered in liquid. Pour the honey and red wine syrup over the pears, cover and bake in the oven for 15–20 minutes @ 190°C/gas mark 5. Remove the pears from the oven and leave to sit in the syrup to cool down.

When they are cool enough to handle, remove the pears from the dish, stand upright on a plate and sprinkle with a little demerara sugar. Drizzle with some of the syrup and serve immediately with the Chantilly cream on page 112.

275–570ml/$^{1}/_{2}$–1pt full-bodied red
wine – approximately
125ml/4floz runny honey
2–3 cloves
1 cinnamon stick – halved
1 tsp mace
75g/3oz caster sugar
8 whole pears

demerara sugar to serve

Choose pears that are ripe but firm so that they keep their shape when cooked, and keep the skin on to give the dish a more rustic look.

The secret of this cake is to pack it so full of ripe plums – top and bottom – that it can be served either way up.

cardamom,
plum and fig
cake

serves 8

Choose plums that are ripe but firm so that they will hold their shape when cooked.

Place the plums and figs in a large bowl with the zest, cardamom and sugar and leave to infuse for 15 minutes.

450g/1lb plums – halved and stoned
450g/1lb figs – quartered
zest of 1 lime
zest of 1 lemon
6–8 cardamom pods – roughly crushed
25g/1oz demerara sugar

Beat the eggs and sugar until the mixture is light and fluffy and forms soft peaks. Add the flour and butter, mixing lightly. Finally, add the ground and flaked almonds, honey and vanilla extract and mix well. If the mixture is a little stiff, add a little milk.

Line a loose-bottomed cake tin, approximately 18–20cm/7–8 inches in diameter, with greaseproof paper. Remove the cardamom pods from the bowl and arrange a layer of plums and figs on the bottom of the cake tin. Pour the cake mixture over the fruit and smooth the surface with a spatula. Arrange the remaining fruit on top of the cake. Bake in the oven @ 180°C/gas mark 4 for 45–50 minutes until the cake is cooked, golden and firm.

4 eggs
175g/6oz caster sugar
250g/9oz self-raising flour – sieved
175g/6oz butter – softened
50g/2oz ground almonds
50g/2oz flaked almonds
2 dsp runny honey
1/2 tsp vanilla extract
2–3 dsp milk – optional

Remove the cake from the oven and sprinkle with a little demerara or dust with icing sugar. Delicious served hot or cold, on its own or topped with yoghurt and honey.

demerara or icing sugar for dusting

A riot of colours and flavours, fruit salad is one of those desserts fit for any occasion — this one is particularly good for picnics as the fruit is packed into an airtight jar. A little liqueur of your choice can also be added to the syrup.

summertime
fruit salad
in a jar

serves 8

fruit salad

Cut the fruit into attractive, even-sized wedges. Remove the skin from the kiwi but leave the skin on the pears, peaches, nectarines and plums.

2 kiwi fruit
110g/4oz strawberries
110g/4oz blackberries
110g/4oz raspberries
2 pears
2 star fruit
2 peaches
2 nectarines
2 red plums
2 yellow plums

fruit syrup

In a large saucepan, gently heat the zest and juice of the orange and lemon. Add the sugar and stir until it is completely dissolved. Bring the mixture to the boil and remove from the heat. Set the pan to one side to allow the fruit syrup to cool slightly, then add the dessert wine, vanilla pod and a splash of liqueur if desired.

When the syrup has completely cooled, place the assorted fruit in a large glass jar, pour over the syrup, seal and chill for at least 1 hour before serving. The fruit salad will keep for up to 2 days in the fridge.

Delicious topped with a little yoghurt or ice cream or the semifreddo on page 104.

zest and juice of 1 orange
zest and juice of 1 lemon
25g/1oz caster sugar
125ml/4floz white dessert wine, e.g. Muscat de Beaumes de Venise
1 vanilla pod – split
2–4 dsp liqueur, e.g. Marsala, Irish Mist or sherry – optional

As so many people today can't digest gluten, I have made this cake without flour. You can also use gluten-free baking powder, which can be found in most large supermarkets.

lemon, apricot
and
coconut
cake

serves 8

Mix the apricots, honey and lemon zest in a bowl. Leave to one side while you prepare the rest of the cake.

Place the sugar and butter in a large bowl and mix until light and creamy. Separate 3 eggs and in a separate bowl whisk together the egg yolks and the remaining 2 whole eggs. Gradually add the eggs to the butter and sugar, incorporating the almonds and coconut between each addition. Next, add the baking powder and mix well. Fold in the apricot mixture.

Now beat the 3 egg whites until they form stiff peaks and carefully fold into the cake mixture. Transfer to a lined cake tin, approximately 23cm/9 inches by 10cm/4 inches or 15cm/6 inches square. Bake in the oven @ 170°C/gas mark 3 for 30–40 minutes until golden, firm and well risen. Remove from the oven and leave to cool slightly, then turn out and serve warm with yoghurt or crème fraîche.

175g/6oz dried apricots – diced
1 dsp runny honey
zest of 1 lemon
225g/8oz caster sugar
225g/8oz butter – softened
5 eggs
225g/8oz ground almonds
175g/6oz desiccated coconut
1 tsp baking powder

oven-roasted
peaches
in lavender and honey
with semifreddo

Semifreddo is a traditional Italian dessert similar to ice cream but much easier to make. It requires no churning and so no fancy equipment – simply pop it in the freezer for a few hours. It has a velvety smooth texture and melts very quickly, which I think is part of its appeal.

Semifreddo can be flavoured with honey, chocolate or fruit. I have added liqueur to this recipe, but be careful not to add more than the stated amount or the semifreddo will not freeze.

semifreddo

Pour the cream into a large bowl and whisk until it is firm and forms stiff peaks. Place the cream in the fridge while preparing the rest of the ingredients.

Beat the sugar and egg yolks in a large bowl until the mixture is thick and pale. Heat the milk in a saucepan until almost boiling. Add the egg yolk and sugar mixture and whisk continuously over a gentle heat until the custard is thick enough to coat the back of a wooden spoon. Add the liqueur, mix well and set the custard to one side to cool.

When the custard is cool, gently mix in the whipped cream. Transfer the mixture to a shallow container and cover tightly. Place in freezer and leave for 3 hours or until the semifreddo is firm to touch. It will keep in the freezer for up to 6 months.

275ml/½pt double cream

150g/6oz caster sugar
4 egg yolks
125ml/4floz milk
2 tbsp liqueur, e.g. kirsch, amaretto, Marsala or sherry

oven-roasted peaches

Lay the peaches in a lightly greased ovenproof dish, cut side down. In a small saucepan, heat together the honey, butter, lavender and water until the butter has melted and all the ingredients are well mixed. Remove from the heat and set to one side for 4–5 minutes to let the flavours infuse.

Discard the lavender sprigs and pour the infused honey syrup over the peaches. Roast in the oven for 15–20 minutes @ 200°C/gas mark 6. Alternatively, place the peaches below a hot grill until the skin is slightly blackened and the syrup is bubbling.

Remove the peaches from the oven or the grill and allow to cool slightly. Using a slotted spoon, arrange the peaches in a serving dish and pour over a little lavender and honey syrup. Top with scoops of semifreddo and serve immediately.

6–8 peaches – halved and stoned
4–6 dsp honey
2 tbsp butter
4–6 sprigs lavender
4 dsp water

A light, refreshing fruit sauce, compote is said to aid digestion after a heavy meal – but still satisfies a sweet tooth!

fresh cherry compote

Place the sugar, water, vanilla pod, lemon zest and juice in a large saucepan. Bring to the boil and simmer for 5 minutes. Add the cherries, grapes and Calvados and cook for a further 1–2 minutes until the mixture has thickened slightly. Remove the pan from the heat.

Remove the vanilla pod. Garnish the compote with mint and serve warm with ice cream or cheesecake.

50g/2oz caster sugar
275ml/^{1}/2pt water
1 vanilla pod – split
zest and juice of 1 lemon
450g/1lb cherries – stoned
110g/4oz seedless grapes (optional)
1 tbsp Calvados
handful mint to garnish

Compote can be made with virtually any fruit – try combining the cherries with grapes, blueberries, apricots or apples.

Calvados originates from northern France and is distilled from cider. Rich, dry and spicy with just a hint of apple, Calvados adds depth to both sweet and savoury dishes and is also a great digestif.

summer fruit compote

serves 6

Place the honey, sugar and water in a large saucepan and stir well. Bring to the boil and simmer for 5 minutes, then add the wine and turn off the heat. Add the fruit to the saucepan and stir gently. Leave the fruit to soften in the syrup. When the compote has cooled, pour into a jug and place in the fridge to chill before serving.

This compote can also be made in the oven. Place all the ingredients in an ovenproof dish and bake in the oven at 180°C/gas mark 4 for approximately 15 minutes.

6 dsp honey – runny or very soft
50g/2oz caster sugar
275ml/^{1}/2pt water
125ml/4floz rosé wine
225g/8oz strawberries – halved
225g/8oz raspberries
225g/8oz blueberries
2 peaches – cut into wedges
2 plums – cut into wedges
2 nectarines – cut into wedges

In France this pudding is baked to welcome in the cherry season. Traditionally made with just batter and fruit, I have added a hazelnut pastry base for even more texture and flavour.

bing
cherry clafoutis

pastry

Place the flour, icing sugar and ground hazelnuts in a bowl. Rub in the butter until the mixture resembles fine breadcrumbs. Add the egg and mix to form a soft dough. Turn out onto a floured worktop and knead lightly to remove any cracks. Roll out the pastry to line a lightly greased flan dish 18–20cm/7–8 inches in diameter and cover with greaseproof paper and a layer of dried beans or lentils to prevent it rising in the centre. Bake in the oven @ 220°C/gas mark 6 for 10–15 minutes. Remove the beans or lentils and the greaseproof paper from the pastry case and cook for another 5 minutes.

200g/7oz plain flour – sieved
25g/1oz icing sugar
50g/2oz ground hazelnuts
75g/3oz butter – softened
2 egg yolks – lightly beaten

filling

Place the milk, vanilla pod and caster sugar in a saucepan over a low heat. Add the egg yolks. Blend the flour with the 2 dsp milk and add to the saucepan. Whisk until the mixture is smooth. Continue to heat until the mixture thickens slightly, whisking continously, but do not allow to boil. Remove the pan from the heat, remove the vanilla pod and set to one side to cool slightly.

Remove the pastry case from the oven and spread the cherries evenly over the surface. Pour over the custard and bake in the oven @ 170°C/gas mark 3 for 30 minutes. Serve warm with the champagne sabayon on page 114.

275ml/1/2pt milk (or milk and cream)
1 vanilla pod – split
25g/1oz caster or demerara sugar
3 egg yolks
25g/1oz plain flour
2 dsp milk
450g/1lb bing cherries – stoned

Bing cherries are large, extra sweet and very dark – almost black – in colour. They are available in large supermarkets from May to early August. You can also make this clafoutis with apricots or peaches.

Mostly used as a marinade for red meat or in salad dressings, balsamic vinegar also works well with fruit, especially strawberries.

baked lemon
cheesecake
with
honeyed balsamic strawberries

serves 8

The best balsamic vinegar comes from Modena in Italy, where its production is strictly regulated. Made from concentrated grape juice, which gives the vinegar its distinctive fruity aroma, it is aged in wooden barrels for at least twelve years. A wide range of young and inexpensive balsamic vinegars are now available in supermarkets, but it is well worth investing in the Modena variety, which is far superior in taste.

balsamic strawberries

Place the strawberries, balsamic vinegar and honey in a large bowl and mix until the strawberries are well coated. Cover the bowl with clingfilm and store in the fridge while you prepare the cheesecake.

700g/1 1/2lb strawberries – halved
2 dsp balsamic vinegar
2 dsp runny honey

cheesecake

Place the biscuits in a plastic bag and crush with a rolling pin to make smooth, fine crumbs. Melt the butter in a saucepan and add the biscuit crumbs and almonds. Stir well – you may need to add a little honey or marmalade to help bind the mixture at this stage.

125g/4 1/2oz shortbread or oatmeal biscuits
75g/3oz butter
50g/2oz ground almonds
1 dsp runny honey or marmalade

Transfer the biscuit mixture to a well-greased, loose-bottomed cake dish, approximately 18cm/7 inches in diameter. Press down and even out to form a base. Leave to one side to cool.

Mix together the cheese, lemon zest, vanilla essence, sugar and cream in a large bowl. Add the eggs a little at a time, stirring continuously until the mixture becomes smooth. Spread the cheese mixture over the biscuit base and smooth the surface. Bake the cheesecake in the oven @ 180°C/gas mark 4 for 1 hour until golden and firm to touch.

700g/1 1/2lb cream cheese
zest of 1 lemon
few drops vanilla essence
50g/2oz caster sugar
125ml/4floz whipping cream – lightly whipped
6 eggs – lightly beaten

Remove the cheesecake from the oven, leave to cool, then chill in the fridge for 1 hour. Using a slotted spoon, top the cheesecake with the strawberries and drizzle with a little of the balsamic syrup. Garnish with sprigs of mint and serve immediately with the Chantilly cream on page 112.

small handful mint

This light and creamy cheesecake is delicious served on its own or with the summer fruit compote on page 106.

honeyed cheesecake

on its own or with the summer fruit compote on page 106.

serves 8

biscuit base

Melt the butter in a small saucepan. Add the honey and biscuits and stir over a gentle heat until the mixture starts to bind together. Transfer to a lightly greased, springform cake tin, approximately 18cm/7 inches in diameter. Press down well and leave to one side to cool.

50g/2oz butter
1 dsp runny honey
150g/5oz almond biscuits – crushed

filling

Beat the eggs and sugar together in a large bowl until light and creamy. Add the honey, Marsala, lemon zest and ricotta and mix until well combined. Pour the mixture over the cooled biscuit base and bake in the oven @ 170°C/gas mark 3 for approximately 1 hour until golden and set. (Don't worry if the cheesecake is still a little soft in the centre.) Remove the cheesecake from the oven and allow to cool. Gently remove it from the tin and serve sprinkled with a little icing sugar.

5 eggs
50g/2oz caster sugar
6 dsp runny honey
6 dsp Marsala wine
zest of 1 lemon
700g/1 1/2lb ricotta
1 dsp icing sugar

This delicious cake is flavoured with orange and almond, then topped with caramelised oranges, nectarines and mascarpone.

seville
orange cake
with caramelised nectarines
and toasted mascarpone

serves 8

the cake

Beat the egg yolks and caster sugar in a large bowl until pale and creamy. Gradually cut in the butter and mix well. Fold in the zest and ground almonds and mix again. Add the flour to the bowl, a little at a time, mixing well with a spatula after each addition. You should end up with a smooth mixture. Whisk the egg whites in a separate bowl until they form soft peaks and carefully fold into the cake mixture.

Lightly grease and sugar a cake tin, approximately 18–20cm/ 7–8 inches in diameter, preferably the springform type as this cake is very soft in texture. Spoon in the cake mixture and even out the surface with a spatula. Bake in the oven @ 180°C/gas mark 4 for 45–50 minutes until the cake is golden and firm to the touch.

3 eggs – separated
175g/6oz caster sugar
75g/3oz butter – softened
50g/2oz ground almonds
zest of 2 oranges
175g/6oz self-raising flour – sieved

the topping

When the cake is almost ready, peel the oranges, remove the pith and pips and cut into segments using a sharp knife. Keep the skin on the nectarines and cut into similarly sized wedges.

Place the sugar and water in a saucepan over a low heat. Stir well until the sugar is dissolved, then turn up the heat and boil rapidly until the mixture becomes thick, syrupy and golden. Add the almonds, oranges and nectarines and mix until the nuts and fruit are well coated. Turn off the heat and leave to cool slightly.

Remove the cake from the oven and prick the surface with a fork. Using a slotted spoon, top the cake with the oranges, nectarines and almonds, then drizzle a little of the syrup over the top and round the sides – the pricks made by the fork will allow the syrup to be absorbed into the cake. Dot the top of the cake with mascarpone and dust with icing sugar. Flash below a hot grill for 1 minute or brown lightly with a blowtorch.

Slice and serve immediately, scooping up a little extra fruit and syrup as desired.

2 oranges
2 nectarines

50g/2oz granulated sugar
2 dsp water
50g/2oz whole almonds
50g/2oz mascarpone
25g/1oz icing sugar

Imported from Spain and North Africa, clementines are perfect for cooking as they are small, seedless and very sweet.

scented
summer clementines

This recipe works just as well without wine – simply replace the wine with a sugar syrup made from 275ml/^{1}/2pt water and 110g/4oz sugar.

All the ingredients and utensils need to be very cold for this recipe, and the cream must be prepared at least 1 hour prior to serving to let the flavour develop. You can vary the quantity of cream used depending on how much you require, but remember, it whips up to double its original volume.

Place the wine, star anise, cinnamon and vanilla pod in a large saucepan and bring to the boil. Add the clementines to the saucepan and remove from the heat. Place to one side and allow to cool and infuse.

Spoon the oranges into a glass serving bowl and drizzle over a little syrup. Top with Chantilly cream and serve immediately.

275ml/^{1}/2pt dessert wine, e.g. Muscat de Beaumes de Venise
1 star anise
1 cinnamon stick – halved
1 vanilla pod – split
8–10 clementines – peeled with pith removed

This cream can be flavoured with chocolate, coffee, lemon, vanilla or a liqueur of your choice.

chantilly cream

Place the cream and milk in a very cold bowl and whisk until the mixture doubles in volume. This should take approximately 3–4 minutes. Add the icing sugar, vanilla essence, water and lemon zest and continue to whisk for a further minute.

Spoon the cream into a serving bowl and place in the fridge for at least one hour to let the flavours develop.

This cream is delicious with the scented clementines and makes the perfect accompaniment to warm desserts such as the oven-roasted peaches on page 104.

150ml/^{1}/4pt double cream
2 tbsp milk – ice cold
2 tbsp icing sugar
^{1}/2 tbsp vanilla essence
1 tbsp water – iced
zest of ^{1}/2 lemon

The ultimate indulgence!

dark
chocolate tart
with champagne sabayon

Place the butter, flour, almonds, sugar and egg yolk in a food processor and whiz until the ingredients bind together to form a soft dough. You may need to add a little cold water to help the mixture bind. Wrap the pastry in clingfilm and place in the fridge to rest for 15–30 minutes.

Lightly grease a shallow, loose-bottomed tin, approximately 25cm/10 inches in diameter. Remove the pastry from the fridge and roll out to line the tin. Trim off any excess pastry and prick the base lightly with a fork. Cover the base with a layer of greaseproof paper and dried beans or lentils to prevent the pastry rising in the centre. Bake in the oven @ 180°C/gas mark 4 for 8–10 minutes. Remove the beans or lentils and paper and cook for a further 5–7 minutes until the pastry case is firm and slightly golden.

75g/3oz butter – softened
125g/4¹/2oz plain flour
25g/1oz ground almonds
25g/1oz icing sugar
1 large egg yolk
1 dsp cold water

Whisk together the eggs, egg yolks and sugar in a large bowl until the mixture forms stiff peaks. Melt 250g/9oz of the dark chocolate and all the white chocolate in the microwave or over a saucepan of warm water. Add the butter to the chocolate and stir gently until the butter melts. Finally, fold the chocolate mixture into the beaten eggs. Mix well.

Sprinkle the remaining dark chocolate and the flaked almonds over the pastry case. Pour over the chocolate mixture and bake in the oven @ 200°C/gas mark 6 for 15 minutes or until set and firm.

Remove the chocolate tart from the oven and allow to cool. Slice and serve immediately with the warm sabayon sauce.

3 large eggs
3 egg yolks
50g/2oz caster sugar
275g/10oz good quality dark chocolate with at least 70% cocoa content – chopped
110g/4oz white chocolate – chopped
50g/2oz butter
50g/2oz flaked almonds – toasted

champagne sabayon

Place the egg yolks, 1 tbsp caster sugar, champagne and lemon juice in a bowl over a large saucepan of simmering water. Whisk for approximately 10 minutes until the mixture becomes thick and frothy and has doubled in volume. Add the remaining caster sugar and flaked almonds to the sauce and mix gently. Transfer to a small jug and serve immediately.

3 egg yolks
2 tbsp caster sugar
6 tbsp champagne
juice of 1 lemon
25g/1oz flaked almonds

I love this combination of spicy ginger and cool, creamy ice cream. Try it served with the dark chocolate tart opposite.

. ginger
ice cream

serves 6

Beat the egg yolks and 2 dsp of the caster sugar in a bowl until the mixture becomes pale and creamy.

Place the remaining sugar, and the milk and cream in a small saucepan and cook over a gentle heat, stirring continuously, until the sugar has dissolved. Gradually add the egg mixture to the pan, still stirring constantly, and continue to heat for a further 5–6 minutes until the custard is thick enough to coat the back of a wooden spoon. Remove the pan from the heat and stir in the fresh ginger.

Allow the custard to cool, then churn in an ice-cream maker. Alternatively, pour into a shallow container, cover securely and place in the freezer, stirring every hour until set to break up the ice crystals.

Remove the ice cream from the freezer 5 minutes before serving and scatter with pieces of preserved ginger.

4 egg yolks
50g/2oz caster sugar
250ml/1/2pt milk
250ml/1/2pt cream
2 dsp caster sugar
2 tbsp fresh ginger – peeled and grated
2 tbsp preserved ginger – finely chopped

quick
toffee apple
ice cream

serves 8

Make the custard base by placing the eggs, sugar, milk and vanilla essence in a saucepan. Stir gently over a medium heat for 5–6 minutes but do not allow to boil. The custard is ready when it is thick enough to coat the back of a wooden spoon. Remove from the heat and set to one side to cool.

Place the sugar and butter in a saucepan and heat until the mixture becomes syrupy. Add the apples and cook until the apples are golden brown but still holding their shape. Remove from the heat, allow to cool, and gently break up the toffee.

Add the custard to the toffee apple and mix well. Churn in an ice-cream maker. Alternatively, pour into a shallow container, cover securely and place in the freezer, stirring every hour until set to break up the ice crystals.

Delicious served on its own or with the warm tarte Tatin on page 116.

6 egg yolks
110g/4oz caster sugar
425ml/3/4pt milk (or milk and cream)
few drops vanilla essence

50g/2oz granulated sugar
50g/2oz butter
2 bramley apples – peeled, cored and sliced

Originally from the French region of Solonge, tarte Tatin is basically an upside down apple pie. Different pastries can be used, but I think this crumbly version works best.

bramley apple
tarte tatin

serves 6–8

The full French title of this dish is Tarte des demoiselles Tatin, named after the two unmarried sisters who invented it.

You can use an oven-proof frying pan for this recipe. However, I do think it is well worth investing in a proper tarte Tatin dish. It's like a frying pan but it's two low-set handles greatly aid the turning out onto a serving plate. Good for pancakes and crêpes as well.

pastry

Place the flour, baking powder, vanilla essence, butter, sugar and egg yolks in a food processor and whiz for approximately 2 minutes until all the ingredients bind together. Alternatively, this pastry can be made by hand. Place the flour and baking powder in a bowl, cut and rub in the butter, then add the sugar, vanilla essence and egg yolks. Mix well until the pastry comes together to form a dough. Wrap the pastry in clingfilm and rest in the fridge for 15–30 minutes.

225g/8oz plain flour – sieved
1/2 tsp baking powder
1/2 tsp vanilla essence
125g/41/2oz butter
25g/1oz caster sugar
2 egg yolks

filling

Mix the butter and sugar in an oven-proof frying pan or tarte Tatin dish until the mixture starts to caramelise. Place the apples rounded side down on top of the mixture in a circular pattern. Cook for 10–12 minutes until the apples are golden in colour and the sugar has turned to caramel. Remove from the heat.

Roll out the pastry to fit the size of the tarte Tatin dish and lay it over the top of the apples, tucking in any excess pastry tightly around the apples. Place the tarte Tatin in the oven @ 200°C/gas mark 6 for 10–12 minutes, then reduce the heat to 180°C/ gas mark 4 for a further 10 minutes or until the pastry is golden and has risen slightly.

Remove from the oven and leave to cool slightly. Using a knife, loosen the pastry around the edge of the dish and place a plate on top of it. Quickly turn upside down so that the tarte Tatin is flipped onto the plate. Serve immediately, topped with the toffee apple ice cream on page 115.

4–6 bramley apples – peeled cored and quartered
50g/2oz butter
110g/4oz caster sugar

vanilla and
almond tart
with rose-scented plums

This panna cotta can also be made with cream and yoghurt. The fruits can be poached on their own or with lavender and rosemary; here I've used my favourite, a combination of cardamom and rose water.

almond pastry

Place all the ingredients for the pastry in a food processor and whiz until they begin to form a dough. You may need to add a little water. Wrap in clingfilm and place in the oven to rest for 15–30 minutes.

Roll out the pastry to a thickness of 1cm/^{1}/2 inch and line a lightly buttered flan dish, approximately 18cm/7 inches in diameter. Trim off any excess pastry. Prick the base lightly with a fork and cover with a layer of greaseproof paper and dried beans or lentils to prevent it rising in the centre. Bake @ 180°C/gas mark 4 for 15 minutes until well cooked. Remove and allow to cool.

175g/6oz plain flour
50g/2oz ground almonds
1 dsp icing sugar
110g/4oz butter – softened
1 egg – lightly beaten
1–2 dsp water – optional

panna cotta filling

Place the cream and sugar in a saucepan over a medium heat. Remove the seeds from the vanilla pod and add them and the pod to the pan. Stir until the sugar has completely dissolved. Remove the saucepan from the heat. If using powdered gelatine, place the powder in a small bowl and add 2 dsp of cold water. Place the bowl over a small saucepan of warm water until the gelatine dissolves into a clear syrupy liquid. Add the gelatine and buttermilk to the cream mixture and whisk until smooth and showing signs of setting. Remove the vanilla pod and pour into the cooled pastry case. Place in the fridge to set for 1–2 hours.

275ml/^{1}/2pt cream
50g/2oz caster sugar
1 vanilla pod – split
25g/1oz gelatine powder
2 dsp cold water
275ml/^{1}/2pt buttermilk

rose-scented plums

Place the rose water, water, sugar and cardamom seeds in a shallow saucepan. Heat gently for 2–3 minutes until the sugar has dissolved, then boil for a further 2–3 minutes to form a syrup. Add the plums to the syrup and poach gently for 7–8 minutes. Do not allow the fruit to break up. Remove the plums from the pan, turn up the heat and simmer for an additional 2–3 minutes to further reduce the liquid.

1 tbsp rose water
150ml/^{1}/4pt water
1 dsp caster sugar
4–6 cardamom pods – seeds only
8–10 plums – stoned

Using a slotted spoon, arrange the plums on top of the vanilla and almond tart and drizzle with a little syrup. Serve immediately, garnished with mint.

sprig mint

Bursting with the flavour of sunshine lemons, this tangy tart always reminds me of long hot summer holidays.

tarte au citron

pastry

Make the pastry by hand in a large bowl. Place the flour, sugar, ground almonds and lemon zest in the bowl and mix well. Cut and rub in the butter. Add the flaked almonds and mix again. Finally, add the egg yolk and water and mix well to bind the ingredients together. You may need to add a little extra water if the dough does not come together. Shape the pastry into a round, wrap in clingfilm and place in the fridge to rest for 15–30 minutes.

Roll out the pastry to line a well-greased flan dish, 18–20 cm/7–8 inches in diameter. Prick the base lightly with a fork and cover with a layer of greaseproof paper and dried beans or lentils to prevent the pastry from rising in the centre. Place in the oven @ 180°C/gas mark 4 and bake for 10–12 minutes. Remove from the oven and discard the beans or lentils and greaseproof paper. Set to one side to cool, then return to fridge to chill for approximately 20 minutes.

225g/8oz flour
25g/1oz caster sugar
50g/2oz ground almonds
zest of 1 lemon
175g/6oz butter – softened
25g/1oz flaked almonds
1 egg yolk
1 dsp cold water

lemon filling

Place the eggs, sugar, cream and lemon zest in a large bowl and whisk well until creamy. Add the butter and lemon juice and whisk for a further minute. Pour into the chilled pastry case and bake in the oven @ 180°C/gas mark 4 for 25 minutes until the mixture is set.

Remove the tart from the oven and allow to cool before chilling in the fridge for 30 minutes.

Serve with crème fraîche for a wonderful summery treat.

4 eggs
150g/5oz caster sugar
150ml/¹/4pt double cream
zest of 1 lemon
25g/1oz butter – softened
juice of 3 lemons

Amaretto is an Italian liqueur with the distinctive flavour of almonds, although it is often made with apricot kernels.

saffron-scented plums
with crunchy amaretto
mousse

crunchy amaretto topping

In a small saucepan, gently heat the water and sugar until the sugar has dissolved, then turn up the heat and bubble for 5–6 minutes until the mixture turns golden and syrupy. Add the almonds and mix well, then turn off the heat and add the amaretto. Stir again. Pour out onto a baking sheet, flatten and leave to one side. When cool, place the mixture in a food processor and whiz to a coarse powder, or place in a plastic bag and crush well with a rolling pin. The crunchy amaretto topping can be made in advance and stored in an airtight container for up to one week.

2 dsp warm water
110g/4oz caster sugar
110g/4oz flaked almonds
dash amaretto

saffron-scented plums

Immerse the saffron in the water and leave to infuse for 3–4 minutes.

Place the sugar and the water in a small, deep saucepan and cook over a low heat, stirring constantly, until the sugar has dissolved. Strain the liquid from the saffron, add it to the pan and stir well. Now, add the plums and toss around to coat well. Cover and simmer for 4–5 minutes, then turn off the heat and allow the plums to cool in the syrup. Using a slotted spoon, arrange the plums in a glass serving bowl and pour over a little syrup. Set four plums aside for the individual glasses.

1 tsp saffron threads
2 dsp warm water
50g/2oz caster sugar
275ml/$\frac{1}{2}$pt water
900g/2lb whole plums

mousse

Beat the eggs and sugar in a large bowl until the mixture is creamy and has almost doubled in volume. Slowly pour in the cream, whisking all the time, then transfer the mixture to a small saucepan. Add the vanilla pod and heat very gently, stirring continuously, for approximately 5 minutes or until the custard mixture is thick enough to coat the back of a wooden spoon. Pour into a bowl and set to one side to cool for 15–20 minutes.

Break down the reserved plums with a fork and remove the stones. Spoon the plums into individual glasses.

Remove the vanilla pod from the custard mixture. Add the mascarpone and mix through. Top the plums with enough mousse to almost fill the glasses, cover with clingfilm and chill in the fridge for 2 hours.

Remove the mousse from the fridge, scatter with the crunchy amaretto topping and garnish with mint. Serve immediately with the bowl of saffron-scented plums.

4 egg yolks
25g/1oz caster sugar
275ml/$\frac{1}{2}$pt double cream
1 vanilla pod – split
200g/7oz mascarpone
small handful mint

Mango is one of my favourite fruits and makes a refreshing, exotic sorbet – I just wish that someone would devise a gadget to remove the stone easily!

mango
sorbet

serves 4–6

Heat the water and sugar in a saucepan until the sugar dissolves, then boil the mixture rapidly for 2 minutes.

Mash the mango with a fork until smooth, then add to the sugar syrup and mix well. Place the mixture in a shallow container, cover tightly and freeze for approximately 3 hours. Remove the sorbet from the freezer occasionally and stir with a fork to break down the ice crystal formation. Serve when set and firm.

225g/8oz granulated sugar
275ml/^{1}/2pt water
2 mangoes – peeled, stoned and cut
into chunks

Blackberries are at their best in autumn but can now be found in the shops almost all year round. Fresh blackberries work best in this sorbet but frozen or canned can also be used.

blackberry
sorbet

serves 4–6

Place the water and caster sugar in a saucepan and poach the blackberries until soft. Set to one side to cool.

Place the water, sugar and lemon juice in a saucepan. Heat gently until the sugar dissolves, then bring to the boil. Leave to bubble for 2–3 minutes. Remove from the heat and allow to cool slightly before adding the lemon zest. Fold in the egg white, add the blackberries and mix gently. Place the mixture in a shallow container, cover tightly and freeze for approximately 3 hours. Remove the sorbet from the freezer occasionally and stir with a fork to break down the ice crystal formation. Serve when set and firm.

2 dsp water
25g/1oz caster sugar
450g/1lb blackberries – well washed

275ml/^{1}/2pt water
110g/4oz granulated sugar
zest and juice of 1 lemon
1 egg white – stiffly beaten

vanilla
crème brûlée
with orange-scented prunes

Whisk the egg yolks and caster sugar until pale and creamy. In a saucepan, heat the cream and vanilla pod until almost boiling. Add the egg mixture and whisk well, taking care not to let the custard overheat. Remove from the heat and pour into 2 ramekins. Arrange in a roasting dish filled with enough water to come halfway up the ramekins. Bake in the oven @ 170°C/gas mark 3 for approximately 30 minutes or until set. Remove from the oven and allow to cool. When ready to serve, sprinkle each ramekin with 1 dsp demerara sugar. Flash below a hot grill or use a blowtorch to heat the sugar until it is browned and bubbling. Set to one side to cool.

3 egg yolks
25g/1oz caster sugar
150ml/¹/4pt double cream
1 vanilla pod – split
2 dsp demerara sugar

orange-scented prunes

Place the prunes in a saucepan with the orange zest and juice, cinnamon stick and caster sugar. Poach gently for 4–5 minutes – just long enough to allow the prunes to infuse and swell up. Remove the cinnamon stick and serve warm or cold with the crème brûlée.

225g/8oz dried prunes
zest and juice of 1 orange
1 cinnamon stick – halved
25g/1oz caster sugar

Prunes are one of those dried fruits that are often forgotten about, and in recent times they seem to have fallen out of favour. I love them because of their fantastic flavour and their versatility. Ideal as a breakfast fruit and great in savoury dishes such as casseroles, I've used them here to create a rustic fruit salad.

Acknowledgements

Over the years I have managed to enlist the help of many talented people, and as we continue to make the programmes and write the books, the list just keeps getting longer.

Thank you to Alan Bremner, director of television at UTV, for his continuing support and guidance, and Orla McKibbin, also at UTV, for her hard work in coordinating the book and the television programmes. A big thank you also to Bernie Morrison, producer and director of the television series, for her tremendous vision. She has that unique art of convincing me I should be working and writing recipes to deadlines only she knows are possible. And to my great crew, who have been with me for years: Sam Christie, Ivan Heslip, Billy Rowan, tape editor Warren York, and Mary McCleave, who has the most incredible energy and enthusiasm you have ever seen.

A special thank you to the publishing team at Blackstaff Press, who do such a great job, and with such ease – or maybe it just seems that way!

I cannot forget my hard-working and very loyal team behind the scenes – Maureen Best, Nan Millar and Vera McCready, and Alison Bell at Peter Mark in Ballymena. I am also grateful to photographer Robert McKeag and food stylist Colette Coughlan.

Many thanks also to Helen Turkington at the Fabric Library, Cookstown and Newbridge, County Kildare; to Paddy McNeill of Beeswax, Kilrea, for sourcing the free-standing dressers and cupboards; to Sally at Floral Designs, Ballymena; to Nicholas Mosse Pottery, Kilkenny; Montgomery Cookshop, Ballymena; Laura Ashley, Belfast; Le Creuset; Lakeland Limited; Star Glass Ltd in Hastings; Poole Pottery in Dorset; Dunoon Ceramics Ltd, Staffordshire; Richardson Sheffield Housewares; Tableware at Pimpernel; to Hilary and Ian Robinson at Presence, Newtownards, for so much hard work in coordinating china, pottery and dishes for the programmes; to Sydney Stevenson Agencies, Bangor; Meyer Prestige; to all the amazing people we met while travelling in the south of France; and to all who contributed to the programme and helped make it such an enjoyable experience.

Thank you all so much.

Index

First published in 2005 by
The Blackstaff Press,
4c Heron Wharf,
Sydenham Business Park,
Belfast BT3 9LE,
in association with UTV

© Jenny Bristow, 2005
© Photographs, McKeag & Co, 2005

Jenny Bristow has asserted her
right under the Copyright, Designs
and Patents Act 1988 to be identified
as the author of this work.
Printed in Scotland by Scotprint
A CIP catalogue record for this book
is available from the British Library

ISBN 0-86540-775-5

www.blackstaffpress.com
www.jennybristow.com